EAST OF THE STORM

Hanna Davidson before the war, age nine.

EAST OF THE STORM

OUTRUNNING THE HOLOCAUST IN RUSSIA

Hanna Davidson Pankowsky

Texas Tech University Press

This book was set in Classical Garamond and Charlesworth. The paper used in this book meets the minimum requirements of ANSI/NISO Z39.48-1992 (R1997).∞

Design by Melissa Bartz

Printed in the United States of America

Library of Congress Cataloging-in-Publication Data
Pankowsky, Hanna Davidson, 1929-
    East of the storm : outrunning the Holocaust in Russia / Hanna Davidson Pankowsky.
       p. cm.
    Includes index.
    ISBN 0-89672-408-5 (alk. paper)
       1. Pankowsky, Hanna Davidson, 1928-   . 2. Jews—Poland—Łódź—Biography. 3. Refugees, Jewish—Soviet Union—Biography. 4. World War, 1939-1945—Personal narratives, Jewish. 5. Łódź (Poland)—Biography. I. title.
DS135.P63P349 1998
943.8´4—dc21   98-35211
                                                              CIP
        99 00 01 02 03 04 05 06 07 / 9 8 7 6 5 4 3 2 1

Texas Tech University Press
Box 41037
Lubbock, Texas 79409-1037 USA

800-832-4042

ttup@ttu.edu

Http://www.ttup.ttu.edu

CONTENTS

To
Helen, Danny,
Jay, Nathan, and Shirit

It is my hope that the path I opened will be easier for you, and that what was unreachable for me will be attainable for you, my most beloved children and grandchildren. You are the substance of my life and the reward for my struggles.

ACKNOWLEDGMENT

In 1993 I took a course in creative writing at the University of Texas, Academic Learning in Retirement program, given by an outstanding teacher and talented writer Gigi Starnes. Only with her skillful guidance and unlimited patience, with her love and understanding was it possible to accomplish this difficult task. I can't say merely "thank you" to a person who gave so much of her time, encouragement, understanding, and friendship. Without you, Gigi, this book would never have been written.

Special thanks to David Bowen, for believing in the work; Judith Keeling, editor at Texas Tech University Press, for her patience, help, and support; and to my daughter-in-law Susan Pankowsky, who compiled the index.

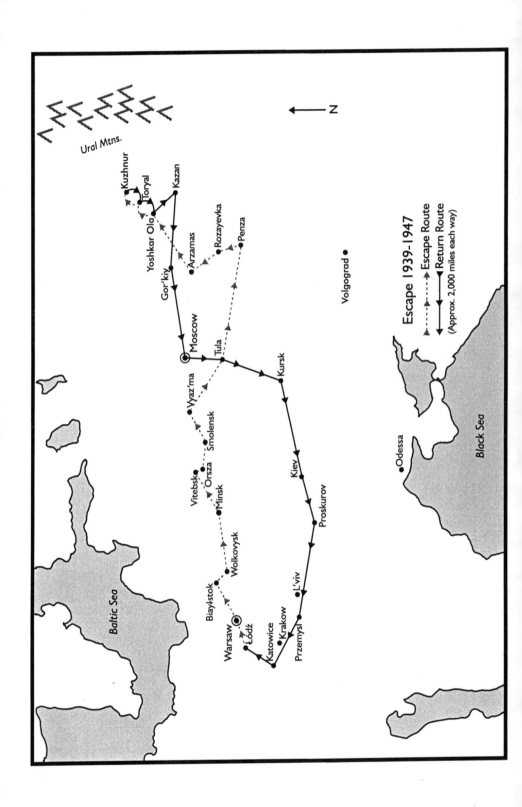

Ural Mtns.

Kuzhmur
Toryal
Yoshkar Ola
Kazan
Arzamas
Rozayevka
Gor'kiy
Penza
Moscow
Tula
Vyaz'ma
Smolensk
Kursk
Vitebsk
Orsza
Minsk
Kiev
Wolkovysk
Proskurov
Bialystok
L'viv
Warsaw
Łódź
Krakow
Katowice
Przemysl
Volgograd

Baltic Sea

Odessa

Black Sea

N

Escape 1939-1947
- - - -► Escape Route
——► Return Route
(Approx. 2,000 miles each way)

INTRODUCTION

Though the memoir form is by definition personal, the story of the experiences of Hanna and her family during the years 1939-1947 is of much broader interest because it is also the story of tens of millions of persons who were driven by the twin forces of politics and war from their homes, their friends and, often, their families. Hanna's story is a story of a girl growing up in a condition of statelessness and with all the personal risk that term implies, with her native language silenced, without extended family, and even without the name with which she was born. She is living at a time and in a place when even one's physical appearance—features and coloring—could betray; she lives in constant fear that someone, somewhere might eventually penetrate her disguise and destroy everything.

The number of people who had to leave their homes in order to escape the tyranny of persecution and war is staggering. Before the outbreak of World War II but after Hitler came to power, about 802,000 Germans (1 percent of the population) had already fled Nazi persecution. About 52 percent of these emigrants had been Jews (one-fourth of them, unfortunately, had escaped to areas that later would be overrun by Nazi troops). During the course of the war, some 60 million Europeans abandoned their homes. Twenty million were forcibly deported to Hitler's camps or to other countries as members of certain ethnic groups. The remaining 40 million, trying to escape the trauma of war or persecution, relocated to safer areas within their own countries (or within the pre-war borders of their countries); only about 17 percent crossed national borders.

In Poland, however, the situation was somewhat different. Although there had been some population movement out of Poland before World War II, such movement greatly increased after Germany's invasion on 1 September 1939. Of 4,508,000 Polish refugees, only 47 percent stayed within Polish borders; 49 percent moved outside the country, and 4 percent escaped both German and

Soviet control. After 29 September 1939, when the Soviets and Germans signed a treaty of friendship that divided Poland into two sectors (with Germans controlling the west and Soviets the east), hundreds of thousands of civilians from western Poland—approximately 300,000 of whom were Jewish—succeeded in escaping eastward to Soviet-occupied territory.

The Davidsons also fled eastward, eventually reaching Białystok, although Hanna and her mother had to make the journey on their own, for Hanna's brother and father became separated from them in the chaos following the German occupation of Łódź. However, with the Germans advancing rapidly at their backs, Hanna and her family found it necessary to move once again, this time out of Poland, to Orsha, near the eastern border of Byelorussia. After a little more than a year, however, they had to go on the road again. Two days after German troops invaded the USSR on 22 June 1941, the Davidsons became part of the government-sponsored series of evacuations of the population eastward. This evacuation included some 400,000 Jews, or around 29 percent of the 1,400,000 Polish civilians and soldiers trying to outrun the German forces. The Soviet Union, however, did not provide a major escape route for refugees either before or after 22 June 1941. The number of people who escaped through the country was small (especially when we consider the millions trapped in Europe who died as a result of military action, starvation, or internment in Hitler's camps). The number who survived, though, was large compared to those who chose to emigrate to western Europe, where only 4.5 percent of Polish Jews eluded the Nazis or the dangers of war.

That the Davidsons decided to place themselves under Soviet control by fleeing east before the advancing German troops is an indication of the extent of their desperation. For Hanna's father's membership in the Bund put his family in grave danger from the Bolshevik communist regime. The situation was complicated by the fact that he had lived in Moscow before emigrating to Łódź shortly after the October Revolution of 1917 and still had immediate family there—family who could be persecuted as relatives of a political criminal. Still worse, since Hanna's father had owned his own business in Poland, he might also come under suspicion as a class criminal, a capitalist who exploited workers. If his identity or his ties to the Bund were discovered, he and his extended family could face imprisonment or Siberia. He would be as despised by the communists for his politics as he was hated by Nazis for his ethnicity.

What, then, was so dangerous about being a Bundist? Organized in the late nineteenth century, the Bund (or General Jewish Workers Bund of Poland, Lithuania and Russia) was a Socialist organization with the twin goals of awakening Jewish workers along both class *and* ethnic lines.[1] Fighting assimilation of Jews into the general culture, Bundists clashed not only with the tsarist government before the October Revolution of 1917, but also with the radical Bolshevik ruling faction after it. When Bundists refused to subscribe to the 21 Points of the Komintern, Bolshevik leaders condemned them as counter-revolutionaries. By 1921, having been destroyed by mass arrests, repression, and slaughter at the hands of the state police, the Bund had virtually ceased to exist in the USSR, although it maintained its influence elsewhere in Eastern Europe.

Twin devils, then, confronted the Davidsons on their eastward flight: at their backs were Nazi troops, and before them was the NKVD (the forerunner of the KGB) holding out the prospect of harassment, imprisonment, or worse. The Davidsons' fears of the NKVD were well founded. Several times during their years in the USSR both Hanna's parents were taken in by NKVD officials for questioning. Once her father had to go briefly into hiding, fearing that his identity and political associations had been discovered by the NKVD. Only in Kuzhnur, far off the beaten track, did they feel secure. It was precisely their fear of the secret police that made the Davidsons doubt whether they had a future in the USSR, and that prompted them to return to Łódź soon after the war. The country in which they had sought haven was, after all, the Soviet Union of Josef Stalin.

Despite the risks involved in living in the Soviet Union, as Polish Jews the Davidsons probably fared better than they would have in most of Europe. Out of a pre-war Jewish population in Poland of about 3,100,000, only about 380,000 Jews, or 11.5 percent survived; of those who survived, 7 percent survived within the Soviet Union. Some Jews who initially escaped into the Soviet Union did not stay there but left for other destinations. Approximately 10,000 (or about 3 percent) reached China or Japan. Another 1,000 reached Palestine by way of the Indian Ocean and the Red Sea. Hundreds reached India, Australia, and New Zealand and a few crossed the Pacific to enter the US, Canada and several Latin-American countries. During July 1942 after mass extermination began in Germany, Soviets allowed an additional four thousand Polish Jews to leave the country through Iran, bound for the Middle East and India. The gamble taken by the Davidsons (and thousands of others like them) had paid off.

By February 1946, however, many Jews like Hanna's family who had lived out the war in the Soviet Union started returning to Poland. Under the terms of the 1945 Polish-Soviet Repatriation Agreement and others that followed, approximately 185,000 Jews were repatriated. Those who had been in the military also returned home, including approximately thirteen thousand Jews who had served in the Polish army organized in the Soviet Union to liberate Poland, six thousand Jews who had been in the Anders Army outside the USSR, and several thousand other Jews who had enlisted in the Soviet army.[2]

By the end of June 1946, when postwar Jewish immigration into Poland reached its peak, about 240,489 had been repatriated. Most, however, did not remain long. Understandably, Jewish survivors had profound fears about their future in Central Europe. They were confronted with the ruins of their lives and evidence of the millions who had died. A simple act like walking down a street could lead (as it led the Davidsons) to the chilling discovery that it was paved with Jewish headstones still bearing the familiar names of dead friends. The uncertain political situation and economic devastation threatened a future filled with hardship, and the reader sees evidence of all these things in Hanna's account of her family's return to Łódź. But perhaps the most compelling reason for the disquiet of Polish Jews was the postwar renewal of anti-Semitism in Poland. The pogrom at Kielce, Poland, on 4 July 1946, in which forty-two Jews were killed and sixty injured, together with the thirty-three other killings that followed (despite the Polish government's efforts to prevent such attacks), scared many. By the end of 1947 only eighty thousand indigenous Jews were left in Poland. This constituted a loss of 97.7 percent of the pre-war Jewish population.

Thus, Polish Jews soon joined the vast numbers of other Europeans after the war who were streaming into resettlement centers. From July 1946 to September 1946, 63,387 Polish Jews arrived in the Allied zones in Western Germany, and more soon followed. It is interesting to note that out of 120,000 Polish Jews who chose to emigrate at that time (one hundred thousand chose to stay at home), only fifteen thousand left Poland as regular immigrants; 105,000 (like the Davidsons) emigrated illegally to Western Germany, Austria, and Italy. By the summer of 1947 there were 247,000 Jews in Germany, Austria and Italy, 73 percent of whom were of Polish origin. After 1947, about 100,000 of an estimated 250,000 Jews living in Assembly Centers in the Western zone of Germany were allowed to emigrate to Palestine to help relieve postwar immigration pressures.

Those refugees who did not wish to be repatriated and were welcome to stay in their host countries were lucky. Far less fortunate, however, were those persons, like the Davidsons, who had to set about the arduous task of obtaining new citizenship. One by one, countries of the world were returning to their pre-war immigration quotas, making it difficult for refugees to move out of the Assembly Centers. In the interim period between leaving their old home and finding a new one, these citizens of nowhere were politically, socially, and economically handicapped; they did not enjoy the security of legal protection, freedom of movement, or access to employment of ordinary citizens.[3] And their problems would follow them to their new homes where they would face twin problems of resettlement *and* reassimilation.

The sheer numbers of people who were displaced by World War II can certainly have a numbing effect on us. To recapture the human dimension, we must listen to the particular voice, in this case to the voice of a girl struggling with forces completely beyond her control or comprehension, a girl who was forced to grow up under the most terrifying circumstances imaginable. Hanna's entire youth—between the ages of eleven and eighteen—was spent in exile and in flight. Yet she pushes aside any temptation to lapse into self-pity and faces even the most terrifying circumstances with a courage that many adults would not be able to maintain. Her strength and maturity have a profound effect upon the reader, as does her eagerness to locate the redemptive detail amid even the most appalling circumcumstances. She instinctively realizes that it is the unchecked human tendency toward stereotype that allows atrocities to happen. She stubbornly recognizes, therefore, the goodness of the German soldier who, when ordered to evict her cousins from their apartment, instead invited them to stay with him—and even offered to adopt their daughter to save her from death in the camps. She recounts as well the bravery of Gentiles like Vala and Jasia who defied the Nazis by aiding or sheltering Jews.

The author's use of a child's voice to narrate the harrowing story of her family and of her people compels us to put aside any preconceived historical understandings and to open ourselves fully to her. It is as if Hanna is sitting in the same room with us as she makes us witnesses of her history and that of several million others. It is her child's voice that dominates the manuscript—a voice, accepting, hopeful, that reminds us that measured personal triumph can sometimes emerge from the depths of historical tragedy.

Mary Maddock
Fort Worth, Texas
Summer 1998

NOTES

1. Bernard Johnpoll, *Politics of Futility: the General Jewish Workers Bund in Poland, 1917-1943*. (Ithaca: Cornell Univ. Press, 1967), p. 23.

2. Israel Gutman "Polant: The Jews in Poland," in *Encyclopedia of the Holocaust* (New York: Macmillian Publishing Co., 1990), p. 1174.

3. Much of the information presented about the post-war conditions of refugees is indebted to Malcolm J. Proudfoot, *European Refugees, 1939-52: A Study in Forced Population Movement* (Evanston: Northwestern Univ. Press, 1956).

AUTHOR'S INTRODUCTION

Digging in the past is a monumental task. Reviving war memories is painful. I undertake this journey in the twilight of my life because the obligation to do so weighs heavily on my heart.

Everyone's story is different, yet everyone's story is the same. We were thrown together in a time out of control, in which unspeakable cruelties and the most horrifying of tragedies occurred. Much of what happened to me and my family also happened to others. It was a hard time, but we did what we had to do in order to survive. Some things I remember, however, I have not seen recorded elsewhere, particularly during the time we lived in Russia.

We who survived were changed forever. We will always remember. The child of fifty-five years ago, that child so terrified by what happened to her, is with me even today. I will try to bring to life those events of long ago, yet which still seem so recent.

Open Letter to Childhood Companions
Who Did Not Survive

My dearest little friends:

For more than fifty years, I've carried your images with me, along with the images of family members who, like you, did not survive the Holocaust. I made a promise: Never forget. I've done what I could, in my way, to remind others. I have spoken to hundreds of children at their schools, and I have told about what happened to you. I have told what happened to me.

You are not here anymore, so it is up to me, as it is up to other survivors, to tell the world. No matter how difficult the task, to be silent is also to be guilty. And so, dearest little friends, I've written about us, about who we were, about who I am.

I write about you, about all of us. I cry and miss you. I cherish you, and always will.

Love,

Hannya

On August 31, 1939, Hitler ordered the invasion of Poland. Early on the morning of September 1, the German Luftwaffe crossed the Polish frontier and began the systematic destruction of Polish airfields, roads, and rail centers. Almost immediately, German ground troops crossed Polish borders, and by September 4 they had already penetrated more than fifty miles into Poland. Two huge fronts of advancing German troops circled much of Poland, successfully preventing the Polish army from stopping the invasion.

The fate of the Polish people was sealed on September 17, when Russian troops moved in from the east, a move made possible by secret clauses in the Russo-German Pact of Nonaggression which had been signed on August 25.

Poland as a nation ceased to exist.

1
HOME IN POLAND

In medieval times, kings and nobles invited my ancestors, along with many other Jews from European countries, to live in Poland in order to develop commerce and build cities. Many families prospered, especially under the rule of King Casimir the Great (b.1333-d.1370). After so many generations of us who were born in Poland, not one single family member remains there today.

I was born in Łódź, Poland, in 1928, to a successful Jewish family. I had my mother's light complexion and my father's grayish-blue eyes and was in awe of my older brother, Kazik. At that time, Łódź was a large industrial city filled predominantly with textile factories. As a child, my main obligation was to attend school and study hard. Once my homework was done, I liked to play, using dolls as models for dresses I designed and made. My favorite was a tiny baby doll that I pretended was alive. For this doll, I created an extensive wardrobe. Reading was my favorite activity, and I was fortunate to have access to many books. I attended ballet classes, and in the winter, ice skating was my favorite pastime. As I skated on icy ponds, I frequently imagined myself as a great ice skating dancer performing for large audiences.

The building in which we lived had been designed by my uncle, Henryk Levinson, who was a prominent architect. Our building was located on the corner of Bandurskiego and Vulchanska Streets. I remember impressive double entrance doors guarded by a porter who lived with his family in a small apartment to the left. To the right was a glass door that could be opened only by residents of the apartments via an interphone.

My parents, Kazik, and I lived on the fifth floor. Our housekeeper, Jasia, also lived with us. The entrance hall led to our living room, dining room, kitchen, and the rest of the house. In the back of the apartment was a bathroom and dressing room, from which a small door led to the attic—a mysterious place, excellent for hiding.

My grandmother, Helen Gutentag, lived two blocks from our home on Bandurskiego Street with her youngest daughter, Ala, a poet. Mother's older sister, Stephany, lived on Piotrkowska Street—just a few blocks away from us—with Uncle Henryk, my cousin Marie, and her husband Frank. Stephany, Mother, and Ala were all born in Łódź.

Mother, Sofia Gutentag Davidson, was born in 1893 into an elite, assimilated family in Łódź, Poland, in the house at 51 Piotrkowska Street, which today is marked as a treasure of outstanding architecture. In this house three generations were born: my grandmother; her four children, including my mother; Kazik and I.

Early in her childhood, Mother's artistic abilities became apparent and she was encouraged to develop her talent. After graduating from gymnasium (secondary school for students preparing to enter a university), she continued her education in Warsaw at the Institute of Fine Arts under Professor S. Majewsky, then later in Munich with Professor Von Vebshits, and finally in Zurich at the Academy of Fine Arts. In 1917, she returned to Łódź and lived with her parents. On the top floor of the building, a room was adapted for her studio, and on a huge table she worked on batiks using hot wax on fine silk or chiseling or etching pieces of ivory or copper.

In the years between 1918 and 1923, she became active in a newly organized artistic and literary group known as the Yung Yiddish (Ing Idisz). This group was founded in Łódź in order to revive Jewish art and was the only important Jewish artistic group during this period of time in the whole of Poland. The group flourished, producing many prominent artists, sculptors, writers, and poets, including Mother, Jacob (Yankel) Adler, Moshe Broderson, Ida Brauner, Dina Matus, and Itzhak Katzelelson. Rooted in the works of Marc Chagall, members of the group produced masterpieces of expressionism, abstract art, and post-expressionist realism. As a child, I listened many times when this group met in our home to discuss the newest trends in art and the continuing problems associated with national art. They were considered the darlings of Łódź society. Much of their work disappeared during the war. What remains is scattered.

Piotrkowska 51 Łódź, where Hanna's maternal great-grandparents lived, and where Hanna, her brother Kazik, her mother, and her grandmother were born.

Mother flourished in this atmosphere. She was an established artist, and then she became wife, mother, and teacher. While she did eventually create many important paintings after the war, all of her early works were lost. She never blossomed again and never fulfilled what began as a most exciting and promising life.

Father, Simon Davidson, was born in 1892 in Chagall's home town of Vitebsk, Lithuania. He was the fifth of six children. At the beginning of World War I, his family emigrated to Russia. He was educated in a Moscow gymnasium where less than one percent of Jews were admitted, and he was fluent in Yiddish, Russian, Polish, German, and Latin. The socialist revolution prevented his family from returning to Poland, but my father escaped and settled in Łódź.

Frada Davidson (1840-early 1900s), Hanna's paternal great-grandmother, in 1908.

Hanna's father, Simon Davidson, with his sisters (left to right) Zina, Fania, and Sima, c. 1910

Pablo Davidson (1860-1921), Hanna's paternal grandfather, in 1919.

Father was a well-known member of Bund, a major Jewish social-ist party in eastern Europe that defended Jewish cultural life and autonomy against Leninism, clashed with Russian and Polish anti-Semitic parties, and fought Jewish assimilation. He was an eternal optimist who always believed everything would turn out fine.

Hanna's parents, Sofia and Simon Davidson, in 1937, in front of their apartment building in Łódź.

Kazik, my older brother, attended a Polish gymnasium for boys called Piłsudski. It was an exclusive school, and admittance was earned with difficulty. The academic standards were extremely high, which required a great deal of study and extensive homework. Some-times Kazik's friends would study after school in our home.

Kazik's hobby was to build radios, and he used all the new techniques of the time. He completed a special radio on which we listened to many stations transmitted from Europe. This radio was connected to anten-nas that had to be disconnected during thunderstorms because of lightning, of which I was extremely frightened. I imag-ined this lightning entering the radio and running into our apartment, burning every-thing along the way.

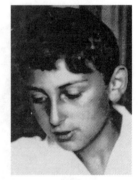

Kazik, Hanna's brother

On rare occasions, Kazik was forced by our parents to take me to a movie show. This was a disgrace to him. He hated to be seen with his little sister by his friends—or even worse, by his girlfriend. During games of tennis he played with our cousin Marie, however, the same little sister would be welcome to pick up tennis balls. In truth, I was very proud of this important function.

Hanna on horseback in a park in Łódź, 1938.

Summer school camp in Tatra Mountains, 1938. Hanna, second from right in back row, and her friend Hania, far right in first row, were the only Holocaust survivors from this group.

Every summer, Mother, Kazik, and I would leave for a two-month vacation in the mountains. Cousin Marie would always go with us. In the middle of the summer, Father came to visit. He, Marie, and Kazik would go hiking and mountain climbing.

In April 1939, cousin Marie and her husband Frank were blessed by the arrival of twin girls, Anne and Sylvia. While I very much enjoyed playing with the babies, by then political tension was growing, and we children were very much aware of it. Our playing was clouded by this tension. Radio broadcasts of Hitler's screaming speeches threatened neighboring countries like ours, and particularly their Jewish populations. There was talk in my family of sending us children to England, but the idea was abandoned.

My school, a private nonreligious Jewish school for girls, held summer camp for the students, as other schools did. Because of the political unrest in the summer of 1939, we didn't go to the mountains. Our camp was instead located close to Łódź. As summer approached, plans were made for our regular vacations. Marie and her baby girls would go to a nearby resort with her mother, Stephany. Mother and Kazik would go to the mountains. Iza and I would go to school camp. Iza, who was my age, came to live with us when Germany expelled Jews of Polish nationality, giving them just ten minutes to vacate their homes. Their businesses, money, homes, and all belongings became the property of Germany and were given to the Nazis. These people were herded onto trains and dropped at the Polish border. They came to Poland with nothing more than the clothes they were wearing. Many of these Jewish families arrived in Łódź with no shelter and no friends. Native Jews offered them hospitality. Iza came to us, and her parents and brother were taken in by another family. Iza learned Polish quickly and called my parents Mama II and Papa II. Iza and I went by buses this time instead of by train, and it took only a few hours to arrive at our destination. The countryside circling our camp was beautiful. A two-story house stood in the middle of a meadow surrounded by forests and a river leisurely flowing at the bottom of a small hill.

Four girls were assigned to each room, which was fine with us because the more of us in a room, the more fun we would have. Our room was on the first floor. We girls numbered the beds, then drew numbers so we would not fight for the same bed. Once this was settled, we made our beds, arranged our clothing, and were ready for a summer of fun.

Early in the mornings, we arose to our exercises in the fresh air. After this, we had breakfast in the dining hall. Later we went hiking in the forest to pick berries. Then we swam, played ball, and rode bicycles. The big meal was served around two in the afternoon, during which discussions of morning events were in order, as were exchanges of interesting findings such as red poisonous mushrooms or bird nests. After this meal, we rested. Our camp became silent. We all had to be in our own rooms, reading or taking a nap. Later we had more activities, such as creative art, singing, running, and playing. We loved to play tricks on each other, like placing undesirable objects in someone's bed or making a hanging ghost out of a sheet to frighten anyone who entered. Many close friendships developed among us.

One week before the end of our vacation, news came of German activities and the whole camp was hastily gathered by our counselors. In fear and silence, we waited to hear dreadful news. "You have to pack your belongings quickly and orderly," our director, Mrs. Rein, said. "The German army is gathering at the Polish frontier."

From the oldest to the youngest of us, we ran to our rooms. In record time, we stood quietly in lines awaiting our buses. Tension mounted when minutes and then hours passed with no sign of buses on the road. Finally they came and we quickly boarded them and were on our way. We left behind camp, sunshine, happiness, and summer. We also left behind our childhood.

Father picked me up from school, greatly relieved to see me back. Mother and Kazik were still not home. The atmosphere in the city was very tense. The radio constantly transmitted news of Germany demanding the return of the Port of Gdansk to them, and of Germans arming themselves to full capacity. Disaster seemed imminent.

When Russia and Nazi Germany signed a treaty of nonaggression on August 25, Poland knew it would be attacked and that war was inevitable. Young men were drafted. Food disappeared from stores as the radio continuously broadcast instructions. Under total blackout, the entire city was submerged in darkness.

In the midst of this disaster, Mother and Kazik finally managed to return home. Iza left to be with her parents, and it was decided that Stephany, Marie, and the twins should stay away from the city for the time being. Marie's husband Frank was drafted and forced to leave. Uncle Henryk stayed in their apartment.

During the last days of August, we had drills for air attacks. Frequent short siren blasts signified the start of an attack. One long blast meant the end of the attack. Our building had a well-equipped bomb shelter in the basement, and we practiced running down there when we heard the signal announcing an attack. We children became accustomed to the drills, and it didn't seem to us that anything new was going to happen.

On September 1, the day that school was scheduled to start, I was awakened at sunrise by the sound of sirens and heard the radio, to which my parents were anxiously listening. Germany had sent an ultimatum to Poland demanding the Port of Gdansk. War was declared! This alarm was real.

Father did not go to work, and I was told there would be no school. We were instructed through the radio to black out any light and cover each window. At the sound of the dreadfully loud siren and many church bells ringing, I dropped my breakfast. The city was in complete darkness, and I was terrified. I held onto my parents, afraid to move. Gently they pulled me and we ran downstairs, unable to use the elevators. When we reached the shelter, it was already full of people. We sat down silently, and a few minutes passed. Then we heard the roaring of approaching airplanes and the terrible sound of guns. I snuggled closely to my parents, hoping that nothing would happen under their protective wings. Finally the air raid was over, and for the time being we were safe.

We ventured to our apartment to eat what was left of our meal. No sooner did we finish eating than the dreadful sound of the alarm screamed once more. So again we ran to the shelter, where we spent a very long day filled with great fear and uncertainty. I refused to go back upstairs and prepared myself to spend the night in the shelter. So passed the first day of the war for me.

The next two days were spent in the same manner. We could hear bombs exploding in the distance, but so far we were safe. On the afternoon of September 4, we were informed by the man from the civil security guard that a gas bomb had exploded nearby. We all grabbed our anti-gas masks, which had been distributed at the beginning of the war. Doors and windows were sealed, and we were instructed to sit down quietly to avoid consuming too much oxygen. The tension was almost unbearable. There was nothing any of us could do but sit quietly and wait. And wait. And wait. This alert lasted for endless hours, but fortunately it turned out to be a false alarm. Stubbornly, I refused to leave the shelter at all. For the next two days and nights, I simply stayed there. The next afternoon during an air attack we heard a terrible explosion, then falling glass and bricks. I still hear the screams of people pleading for help. Several houses around us were hit by bombs. One was cut in half as if with a knife, and others were completely destroyed. There were many wounded and dead.

On the fifth day of the war, we heard rumors that German soldiers were approaching. And then the air raids stopped. I remember an eerie feeling—no more sirens, no more running to the shelter. We all wondered what to do, what the next step would be.

It was decided that our family would leave Łódź in Uncle Henryk's car and that we would pick up Stephany and Marie and the twins on our way out. Grandmother Helen and Aunt Ala had to stay behind because Ala had an ear infection with a high fever and was unfit to travel. Father ran to Uncle Henryk's, and when he reached their apartment, their tearful housekeeper opened the door. "Mr. Levinson was forced to leave," she said. "A Polish officer confiscated his car, and he himself was forced to drive the officer west, away from the approaching Germans." Later we learned that he was stopped by Russian authorities, who confiscated his car.

This was Wednesday, September 6, early in the morning. As we stood on the street in front of our house awaiting Father to come back with the car, streams of people started passing us. "What is happening?" we asked.

"The Polish military authority ordered all men up to the age of fifty to leave for Warsaw," was the answer. "German tanks are about sixty kilometers from Łódź."

Then we saw Father pushing himself toward us through the crowd. "We have to leave," he said. His face was pale and his eyes were filled with pain. There was no time for consultation, no time for hesitation.

All men were drafted, so Father and Kazik prepared to leave. Quickly they put a few changes of clothes in their backpacks. In minutes, we were again in the street, and I felt Kazik hug me. Mother cried and held him close to her as Father picked me up in his arms, hugging me tightly. Then I found myself standing on the street, holding Jasia, our housekeeper, by the hand, watching Father and Kazik disappear around the corner. "Don't go," I yelled. Tears rolled down my cheeks until I couldn't see anymore. "Don't leave us," I cried. But they were already gone.

Jasia hugged me and Mother tightly. "Don't cry," she told me. "Germans don't like crying girls."

Slowly we returned to our apartment. Had it really been only six days since the war started?

It seemed that as we entered our apartment the first German troops entered the city. We could hear them singing in tune to their heavy boots making steps on the pavement. Soon the first order came: Everyone must line up on the street to welcome the German army. We were told to smile and to cheer. Armed police, with bayonets pointed at us, were there to make sure we obeyed this order. There was nothing else to do but stand and cheer. Finally we were allowed to return home.

The next day, Stephany, Marie, and the twins returned. Marie was in a terrible state of mind. She was terrified of being without Frank. Iza, who had no place else to go, returned to us.

The first acute problem was simply to get food. As soon as the Germans entered Łódź, posters were hung in grocery stores forbidding the selling of food to Jews. Anybody helping us would be punished. There was to be no food for us.

This is when Jasia began to hunt for bread and something to eat for us, exposing herself to great danger. Not being a Jew, she was able to obtain food. She had worked with us for a long time taking care of me while my parents were involved in many cultural activities. I remember frequent reunions held in our house when guests would play with me and hold me in their laps. I learned much from these great people about art, music, literature. Once I sneaked from my bed and hid myself under a table and, unnoticed, listened to their debates until I fell asleep. I was awakened by the noises of everyone's frantic search for a child who had disappeared. It was Jasia who took me back to my room.

Jasia stayed with us until the end. It was she who found food for us when selling even bread to Jews was forbidden. It was she who tried to protect us, not even thinking about the danger to herself. This is how I remember Jasia, for her loyalty.

Life in the streets began to flow slowly and seemed almost normal, except for us Jews. It was decided that children should continue their education. As I walked to school on the first day back, I passed a German school and I could not believe what I saw. From every single window from the eighth or ninth floor, enormous flags were hanging, slashes of red with a white circle and black swastika. The school was illuminated, and flowers were everywhere; it was very festive. German children were singing and laughing. They were all dressed well and each wore an arm band, red with a white circle and swastika.

"Hey, Jew," I heard somebody calling. I turned around. How could he know I was a Jew? Maybe this boy, who was about my age, saw the fear and terror in my eyes. "Hey, Jew," he repeated. "Carry my books."

I refused. Immediately an SS soldier appeared. "Do what you are told," he ordered. "We'll teach you obedience, you Jew."

I did as I was told. I carried this boy's books, as well as mine. At the entrance of his school, he grabbed them from me and happily ran to class. Mother was not far behind me, but there had been nothing she could do. She took my hand and we ran the rest of the way to my school. This first day of school in September 1939 was nothing like our previous years. Subdued and silent, we went to our classrooms. There was a great deal of exchanging impressions and emotions . . . and fear.

Our school consisted of kindergarten, six years of elementary, four years of gymnasium, and two years of lyceum (continuing secondary schooling)—thirteen years altogether. Ours was a standard for all the schools in Poland. We had about five to six hundred students, most of us beginning at age five and continuing until we finished, usually at age seventeen or eighteen. It was a beautiful multistory building, with elementary school and first-year gymnasium on the second floor, separated by a hall. I remember a large auditorium and a physical fitness hall. The third floor was occupied by the remainder of the gymnasium classes and the lyceum. The top floor contained a laboratory for chemistry and physics. Every grade had its own room. We all wore uniforms. The elementary girls had marine outfits, and the older students wore navy blue dresses. Gala dress was a white blouse and blue skirt for everyone. Each school had a design number, and ours was 217. The number was embroidered in silver on blue for gymnasium and gold on red for lyceum. Ours was an old school in which many generations of girls had been educated, and which had produced many talented women. Some of my friends who would have joined this group included Runia, an extremely gifted girl who composed beautiful poetry filled with very profound thoughts that we couldn't understand, and Annet, who drew and painted remarkable pictures.

Our school was taught by an association of teachers to which Mother belonged. She, of course, taught art. There were twenty to twenty-five girls in each room. A room teacher who served as an advisor stayed with the same class throughout. Mother was a room teacher in one of the gymnasium classes.

Runia (left), who did not
survive, and Hanna in 1937.

16

Hanna, seated center front, in white pinafore, was the only survivor of her kindergarten class.

School discipline was rigid. We wore uniforms and no jewelry was allowed. During the class, hands had to be at our backs. There was no talking or standing without permission. There was room for mischievous children, however. When my friend Hania and I were in charge of the maps for geography, we had to bring requested ones from the storeroom. To take extra time away from our lessons, we brought the wrong map. The first time our teacher let it go and we went out again to bring the correct map. After the third time, though, we were promptly sent to the director's office after which we acquired the proper knowledge of each map's location.

When I was in the first grade, our school celebrated its fiftieth anniversary, which was attended by all the staff, students, parents, and friends. Our school flag was to be honored by having a commemorative gold plaque nailed to its post. Being the smallest and youngest in the school, I was accorded the honor of this task. I walked first at the procession, wearing my gala uniform with a navy blue ribbon in my hair. When we reached the stage, the flag was put on the table. Now was the important moment for which everyone was waiting. I stepped forward and picked up a hammer, which I had to hold with both hands. Then I approached the table. When I lifted my hands, I could not reach the flag. I was too little. At that moment, someone picked me up.

"Now you can do it," I heard.

I looked around and saw that it was our director who held me in his arms. Everybody applauded the school's youngest and oldest. What a beautiful moment that was.

2
THE GERMAN INVASION

In the third week of September, Warsaw fell. With the Polish army destroyed, Poland ceased to exist, and was divided according to the German-Russian pact.

Sixteen days after the Germans entered our city, September 22, was my birthday. On that day, I found a little black book with Father's handwriting in Yiddish and Polish. I realized it was his diary. Tears rolled down my cheeks as I read his words on one of the pages: "September 22. A precious little baby was born today, a little girl, my wonderful daughter. I am so happy . . . I am a father." Although Father was not with me on that day, I felt he was sending me a message: "Be strong and brave; we have to survive."

Later, Mother took me in her arms and held me tightly. We stood for the longest time like this. Then she said, "Happy birthday. I have something for you," she said and handed me a small package. I opened it and was delighted to find one of her creations, an ivory circle, about two inches in diameter and about a half an inch thick, with a small sculpture of an exquisite butterfly with her wings spread. On the upper left portion of the circle were petals of a small flower which attracted the butterfly with an aroma that was almost perceptible to me. With her wings expanded, the butterfly was in motion trying to reach the flower's sweet nectar. The veins on her wings were so delicately carved that they almost pulsed with life. I held it in my hands and saw myself as the ivory butterfly, flying away in spring and sunshine and happiness. Magnificent, glorious ivory butterfly, how beautiful you were!

"It's a brooch," Mother said, "and will be framed in gold. For now it is without its frame, but one day you'll be able to wear it."

I never wore my brooch, and neither did I ever hold Father's diary again. I am sure his diary was destroyed, but I am also sure that someone somewhere in Germany has my beautiful butterfly.

We spent much time with Stephany and Marie and the twins, the adults discussing what steps to take next while the children stayed quiet. Marie, who was very young at the time, felt the heavy responsibility of her twins. It was very difficult to find a way to feed the girls. The wet nurse who helped in the beginning was now gone, and Marie did not have enough milk for both girls. She was slipping deeper and deeper into depression. It was a very difficult time for her, but the twins were developing beautifully. They didn't look alike at all. As a matter of fact, one would hardly think they were sisters. Sylvia had black hair and brown eyes, while Anne had blond hair and blue eyes.

During this time, we didn't know the fate of our men. We knew that Henryk was heading for Lvov (now L'viv), that Frank was a soldier somewhere, and that Kazik and Father were supposedly in Warsaw. We heard news on the street that the Polish army was almost destroyed and that Lvov had fallen into Russian hands.

The underground news continued to be passed from person to person. It was said that Warsaw was completely destroyed, that not a building stood undamaged. Dead, wounded, and dying men, women, and children lay on the streets without the possibility of any help. Very few managed to come back to Łódź. Kazik and Father were not among them. At this time, there was only a remote possibility of their still being alive. We held on to this idea desperately.

One day a neighbor from the floor below came to our apartment. "I was asked to leave my apartment immediately," he said. "I was not allowed to take anything with me. Please let me in." His apartment would now be occupied by a Gestapo officer. From then on, he lived with us. We knew that the same thing could happen to us. The desperation and hopelessness of our situation became more pressing. This was the first eviction, but many more followed. Now we had to find food for seven people: Grandmother Helen, Ala, Mother, Iza, myself, Jasia, and our gent. Somehow Jasia was able to find meager provisions for us, but hunger was our constant companion.

We were starved for world news since we were constantly fed Nazi propaganda. Our only resource was the radio. Every day, about six in the evening, it was possible to hear news on the British BBC. There was only one problem: we were forbidden to listen. The penalty was arrest or death.

Nevertheless, at dusk we gathered around the radio. Grandmother Helen and Ala, Mother, our gent, Iza, and I held our breath as we turned the volume very low and listened. Every bit of news was absorbed to be discussed and passed on later. One of us would guard the front door to our apartment, listening for any movement on the staircase. For a long time we had no problem and were able to absorb news like fresh air.

One day, almost at the end of a program, we heard a soldier's heavy boots stomping up the stairs. We immediately turned off the radio, but to our horror, we found that the radio was still hot from being turned on. It was impossible to fool the Gestapo. They knew the meaning of a hot radio in a Jewish home at this time of day. Quickly we poured some cold water on it, drying it immediately, and pretended to play a game. With terrible tension and resignation, we waited in darkness for the fatal moment to come. Seconds felt endless. We held our breath, and then the horrible sound stopped. We waited for a few minutes, expecting the renewed sound of climbing feet. There was not a sound! We waited a little longer, and still all was peaceful. Unbelieving, we did not move for another half hour. Only then did we realize that we had escaped this time. We did not stop listening to the news, however. It was our only connection with the outside world and the need for it was too strong.

Systematically, one step at a time, humiliation, starvation, deprivation, and persecution ruled. A notice was posted that from now on Jews of all ages had to wear yellow stars. I wore a yellow band with a black Star of David that had the word *Jude* in the middle. I had to wear it on my left arm, above my elbow. Once marked, we were easy to recognize, and walking on the street became hazardous. If any German was in our path, we had to step aside and let him or her pass by. On many occasions we were pushed and beaten.

Once, coming home, I saw a car to which an old Jewish man was attached like a horse. On top of the car sat a German soldier. He whipped the man, ordering him to pull. The automobile was too heavy, and the old man could not move it. More lashes fell on him until he was bleeding badly. All this was watched by other Germans, who were laughing. I walked on with my head down, not looking, and trying not to cry. I finally reached home, shaking and sick to my stomach.

To maintain life, we continued normal routines as much as possible. Mother continued contacts with her friends, and we visited them sometimes for short periods of time. The family Blaustein had two sons: Runek, who was Kazik's age, and Kuba, who was about my age. Runek left during the summer for Italy to continue his education in the university, and he had not been heard from since. Kuba and I played together as our mothers talked.

We children continued going to school. On the way to school, I passed the house of my one of my friends, Ruth. She waited for me, and we walked the rest of the way together. Ours was no longer a carefree walk. Schooldays were kept as normal as possible. Our desks seated two girls, and since early years, I had always sat with Hania, my best friend, on the front row. But again, the atmosphere was different. There was no laughing and playing anymore. Instead, discussions of our future were in order. We all knew that our world had changed, but how much and in what ways we did not know.

New posters appeared all over the city. First, a curfew was imposed. From now on, Jews could not be on the streets after dark. All activities had to stop. No more visiting friends in the afternoons. School days were shorter. Now we had to be careful to be at home well before dark. Visiting Stephany and Marie was difficult.

With every new restriction, we had the illusion that this would be the last one, that nothing more could happen to us. How could it be otherwise? But this exactly was the German philosophy—slow strangulation, humiliation, and starvation until spirits are broken and the physical condition of the body is destroyed. Then any possibility of defense and rebellion are gone.

Soon afterward, more posters appeared. To our horror, Jews were forbidden to walk or cross Piotrkowska Street, which divided the city.

And so we lived. Then a high-ranking German officer and his aide moved into Marie's apartment. He was an educated, old-generation German who did not completely support Hitler. Stephany and Mother had been educated in Munich and spoke excellent German, so Stephany would have long conversations with him. He apologized profusely for his actions and graciously allowed Marie and her family to stay in one room for the time being.

This German officer was generous with Stephany and Marie, considering the Nazi stance toward Jews. One day when we visited with Marie, he let us know that they had one whole day to vacate their house and belongings. "It is forbidden for a German to stay in the same home with a Jew," he said with embarrassment. Then he added, "Would you permit me to take one of your twins—Anne? My wife will be delighted, and it is a shame that such a beautiful child should die."

It is almost impossible to absorb such a statement, and even less to have to choose to save your baby's life by abandoning her and putting her in German hands. Yet Marie hesitated only a second. She picked up Anne, holding her tightly. "What happens to us will happen to her," she said. She would not leave her daughter.

We helped them pack two suitcases of the most-needed things. We put the children in the stroller (not forgetting the yellow band on top of the little blanket), put coats on, and slowly walked out, not even looking back as the door closed behind us. They relocated with a distant relative in a part of town with a mostly Jewish population.

We saw many people moving. All over the city, Jews were forced to abandon their houses and possessions accumulated during a lifetime. Elaborate silver candlesticks to be lit during the holidays, jewelry, art, dishes, crystal, furniture, family pictures, everything usable was confiscated and ended up in German hands. Everything, except books. Books were damaging to the human mind—thousands of books were thrown into fires and destroyed.

Heavy at heart, Mother and I returned home. Our group was there, waiting for us. We sat down to a dinner of soup with a few potatoes, a little of some kind of fat, scarce carrots and onions swimming freely in a pot filled with water. We were thankful for today's meal, hoping we would have something to eat tomorrow.

Visiting Marie was very difficult, as it was with our friends. The Blaustein family was living in a section of the city that later became a ghetto. We visited them once and learned that Mr. Blaustein had had a heart attack. As Mrs. Blaustein cried and talked with Mother, Kuba and I also talked. Before sunset Mother and I ran home.

During class at school one day, we smelled smoke. From the windows, we saw flames coming from the oldest and biggest synagogue, located half a block from our school. Teachers tried desperately to calm us, but the sight was too terrifying. Old and young Jewish men were grabbed from the street and forced to pour gasoline on the building, stimulating the fire. In a matter of minutes, the whole synagogue was in flames. Passersby stopped and watched in horror, moving their lips in silent prayer. The building started to fall apart. Windows cracked and walls crumbled.

On top of this synagogue, close to the roof, were large, white marble tablets with the Ten Commandments inscribed on them. Fire completely consumed the synagogue, but these tablets stood untouched. Today they are standing in the same place, contrasting with the skeleton of the black remains of the destroyed structure described in the documentary film *Shoah* (*Holocaust*). These tablets stand as a silent monument: The destruction of six million Jews could not destroy Judaism.

Newspapers printed pictures accusing Jews of destroying their own synagogue. The Jewish community was billed for the gasoline used for the fire.

Our education continued, as the school was still open. Circumstances were the worst we could have imagined—freezing rooms, empty stomachs, the sorrows of the dying and the dead all around us. Still we continued to gather. Then came the order to abandon the school building. It was needed for German use. As we came to school that last, terrible day, lessons were abandoned and we were told our beloved school was no more.

We relocated and shared a building with another school. Our classes started in the afternoon, which brought two complications. First, we had to be home before dark, which gave us only four hours of lessons. The most serious complication, though, was the location of the building. It was on the other side of Piotrkowska Street, which we Jews were forbidden to cross. In order to get there, we had to walk almost across town. As autumn turned into winter, icy winds blew on our faces and went through our bones. Empty stomachs growled. Tired, cold, and hungry, we had a very long way to walk. But still, no one missed a day of school.

The streets became increasingly unsafe. On many occasions, the SS would arrest Jews from the street and they would never be heard of again. With no reason, the Gestapo would hang victims from street lamps, leaving them for days for everybody to see. Religious Jews who resisted beatings had their beards shaved by soldiers who laughed at their accomplishments. All this was done on the streets, in public view.

Terrifying raids to take children became a style of the Nazis. Choosing streets and houses at random, soldiers would block entrances with trucks. Then children were taken from their homes—babies, toddlers, young children. Parents were beaten to unconsciousness trying to save their children, but they could not. These children were thrown into the trucks and driven away and killed.

When I first started wearing my yellow star, I was proud because I was proud to be a Jew. My pride was mixed with fear. Now, only my fear remained and I wished not to be a Jew anymore.

In spite of the terror, we continued our daily routines as closely as possible. One particularly cold day, it was almost dark when Hania and I started home from school. I remember discussing with her how easy it would be to get home by crossing Piotrkowska Street. And after all, why not? All our lives we walked and shopped on this street. "Let's do it," I urged. "Let's cross Piotrkowska."

In no time at all we were on the sidewalk of the street. All of a sudden Hania started screaming: "Germans, Germans, Hanna! Come back, come back."

But I was already on the street, paralyzed with fright. Instantly, two SS men screamed, "*Jude!* Jew crossing the street!" I saw them take their weapons from their shoulders and aim. I ran forward and crossed the street as they shot at me. To this day, I do not know how it is possible that the bullets didn't hit me. I ran to the first entrance of some kind and hid. I listened to the sound of boots running on the pavement around me. Only because I was so small was I able to escape being found. Hania turned back in time and safely ran home.

Much later, completely numb, I finally ventured from my hiding place and ran all the way home. When I arrived, breathless and white as a ghost, my only answer to Mother's questions was, "I am cold and hungry." No one ever knew about this incident. I was too afraid to tell about it. Part of me died that day. I was alive, and yet I was not. I felt that our daily routines were only mechanical movements without any sense at all. I was angry and bitter. Most of those close to me could not understand my state of mind or why I behaved differently.

Rumors started circulating that we'd soon be forced to go to the ghettos. Everyone understood that this meant the beginning of the end for us. What end, no one knew, nor could even imagine.

Then we got news from Father. Someone who managed to return from the part of Poland occupied by the Soviets contacted Mother with the news that he had seen Father and Kazik in Białystok and Henryk and Frank in Lvov. It was hard to believe! I have no words to describe the joy of knowing they were alive. I believe that was the time that the idea of escaping formed in Mother's mind. The question was, how to execute an escape? Later I learned that Father had left some merchandise in his warehouse and Mother was able to sell it quietly.

I was not aware of any preparation preceding our escape. When I returned from school one day, Mother told me that Mrs. Blaustein and Kuba had visited us and they were very upset at not being able to see me, but since it was getting so late, they had to go back home. I did not make much of it. I did, however, wonder why their visit was so late in the day. The next morning Mother told me that we would be leaving Łódź at noon.

I went to Ruth's home because she was sick and not in school. I could only say, "I am leaving." It was understood by us all what that meant. The whole family was around me, crying and hugging. Finally we had to say that dreadful goodbye, and then I left. My next stop was at Marie's. Stephany knew why I was there, so words were not necessary. I picked up Sylvia and Anne, big babies by now, and started to play with them, and Stephany finally had to stop me. I couldn't let go of the babies, I just couldn't. Marie picked them up and took them away from me, then she held me tightly. Stephany, too, and none of us had words.

Suddenly Marie said, "Run now, run fast," and almost pushed me out the door. All of us were sobbing.

Approaching Grandmother Helen's home was almost unreal. She, too, knew the reason for my visit. Ala knew as well. Grandmother was sitting on the sofa when I arrived, and I climbed onto her lap and embraced her. She held me very tightly with both her hands and sobbed.

"Don't worry," I said. "We will be back soon."

Her grip tightened a little. "No," she whispered. "I'll never see you again."

I hear her words in my mind, even today. I don't remember leaving their home. I believe I was in a state of numbness, detached from reality. Because of my young age, I may have been unable to comprehend the gravity of the situation, but I knew it was very serious.

It was still early in the day when I returned home. Mother moved quickly and told me what to do. I put two dresses on myself, a sweater, two pairs of heavy socks, and a coat. Just before leaving, Mother hung on my neck a chain with a gold locket. In our family tradition, this locket was supposed to be mine on my fifteenth birthday. I remember protesting that I was too young, but Mother just hugged me. I also wore a wristwatch given to me by Uncle Henryk, who used to make gifts of them. This watch I still have.

Jasia, Iza, her parents, and our gent were in the house as we were preparing to leave. At the last minute, Iza's parents begged Mother to take Iza with us. But this was not possible. Mother had obtained, through "smugglers," as they were called, false documents with fixed names showing that we were Christians, a mother and daughter, on the way to see her family. Iza was a pretty girl with typical Semitic features, and she spoke Polish with a very heavy accent. It would be impossible for her to pass as a Polish Christian child, even if she had papers.

The act of escaping carried only a two percent possibility of surviving. Mother was accused of going to certain death with no right to take a child with her, and she was advised to leave me behind. Being detained and killed by Germans was not the only danger. Being exposed to the bitterly cold winter during a difficult journey was also considered too dangerous. Under these pressures, Mother decided that Iza would be safer with her parents. She felt she was taking her own daughter to a probable death. She could not do this to someone else's child.

3
OUR ESCAPE

We left our home with only the clothes on our backs. Our departure was quick because it was too emotional and too painful to prolong. We walked through the door, leaving behind everything and everyone. Only later could I understand Mother's true act of heroism, to go alone with her young daughter into a tremendously hostile world.

Barely half an hour after we left, the Gestapo entered our apartment looking for Mother. They had launched raids on intellectuals, scholars, artists, and teachers, and my mother was on their list.

We walked to the place indicated by the smugglers. Their role was to move persons from one place to another, illegally. Smugglers strictly were opportunists, taking advantage of situations in order to make money. They should not be confused with the many men and women who risked their lives to save others. Many of us, however, needed the smugglers.

There was a truck waiting for us. After brief words, I was informed of my newly assumed name, destination, and place and date of birth. I was told that under no circumstances was I to reveal my real name. Discreetly we removed our yellow bands. We had to pretend to be Catholic Poles now, which brought the terrible danger of being recognized by someone and denounced. We got into the truck and kept our heads down. The driver sat behind the wheel and started the motor. He drove through the streets as quickly as possible. I don't remember feeling too much at that time but a mixture of gladness to leave behind Nazi terror and sorrow to leave behind family and friends. Yet I was told not to cry and to have a face indicating a trip to visit relatives in the country.

At one point we were stopped by the Gestapo for inspection and ordered off the truck. Desperately trying not to panic and lose control of myself when I was separated from my mother, I was taken to a room by an enormous German woman and ordered to take off my clothes. I was shaking, but obeyed orders. She searched all my body looking for hidden treasure, but there was none. Stoically, I gave correct answers to her questions. I must have looked quite innocent with my great big eyes, pretty face, and two typically Polish braids tied with ribbons, because she let me go. I got back into the truck and sat incapable of moving a muscle. After a long wait, Mother was freed, too. She was also stripped, interrogated, and released. Before long, our driver appeared, and we were on our way again. Only now can I imagine what was going on in Mother's mind during our brief separation. What torture it must have been for her, not knowing my location, my behavior, or what my tormentors were doing. What tremendous willpower, self-control, and courage she had not to scream and demand her child. Her calm demeanor saved us that day.

We drove for long hours on bumpy country roads, avoiding towns whenever possible. We were heading east to the German-Russian border, hoping to cross to the part of Poland now occupied by Russia. Our destination was Białystok, a city in which a few lucky refugees found sanctuary. My parents had good friends there, the Ravin family, who had moved to Białystok before the war.

We slowly progressed closer toward the River Bug, which was the dividing line at the border. Merciless wind and cold tormented our tired and hungry bodies. Night was approaching, with the shadows of trees moving gracefully, constantly reflecting on the white of the snowy road. The trees became more and more numerous until we reached the forest. The only thing that could be heard was the roaring motor which disturbed the snow-covered silent world. Then the truck stopped and we were told it would not go any further. We were very close to the partition line, but still on the German side. We had to get out of the truck and continue on foot. The truck just turned around and drove back, leaving us in the deep forest with the darkness of night around us.

By now, we were completely exhausted, terribly cold, and hungry. Mother stepped on a rock and fell heavily. I helped her stand with my heart beating furiously. What would I do if she was hurt?

Fortunately, she was fine. I held her arm and she leaned on me as we started to walk again.

We walked a long time. Then, suddenly we heard shots. The bright light of a searching flare could be seen in the distance, illuminating the forest. At the same time, we heard the barking of search dogs. These were German patrols looking for escaping Jews. We could even hear the yelling of SS soldiers.

We threw ourselves to the ground, instinctively seeking protection and covering our bodies with snow. We lay completely immobile, not daring even to breathe. I have no recollection of time passing. It was a long time, I believe. Then we could see the light fading slowly away from the sky. The barking dogs were further and further from us. The SS voices faded in the distance. It took us a very long time until we ventured to continue walking again. Once again, we had tricked death. If the SS had found the two of us, a woman and a girl, there would have been no mercy for us.

Our progress was slow. Because we were completely exhausted by now, the march was very difficult, but we followed a narrow path on the snow formed by the many footsteps of previous refugees leading us to the river. Eventually the forest became thinner and distances between trees longer, until we reached an open meadow, in the middle of which was a half-frozen river. When we got close enough to see the river, the view of the silver ribbon sparkling in darkness brought relief to our tired eyes. We had finally reached the River Bug.

We spotted a boat on the river bank that we hoped was the boat the smugglers had arranged to take us across to safety. We saw figures of people, but there was something wrong. It seemed as though these people were fighting among themselves, and we heard the voices of obviously drunken men. Not daring to come too close, we went only to the point at which we could distinguish voices. It was apparent they were fighting about who was going to cross with the boat and collect the money from us. We had no choice but to advance toward them, hoping for the best. At the end, the strongest man won. Two went away, and the other two approached us. They were native farmers trying to supplement their income by taking people across in the boat because there was no bridge over the river. Mother gave them money, not knowing the outcome. We were hopeful, though, because we saw no Germans around.

At last we were led to the frozen and slippery river bank and helped into the boat. To call it a "boat" is to give it too much importance. It was in very sorry condition; water leaked badly, and there was no place to sit except on the wet bottom. We were told to dip icy water out constantly with small buckets. At that moment, however, this "boat" seemed to us like a magnificent piece of equipment that would take us safely away from danger.

The rowers asked us to bend down so we would not be seen. The Germans would shoot us, and the Russians would turn us back. There was complete silence, but I remember the splashing of the rowers as they dipped the oars into the water.

It was late at night when we reached the opposite shore. With a sigh of relief, we stepped on the soil that was now in Russian hands. Not too far was a Polish village, to which we directed our steps, seeking the house the smugglers had told us to find. This part of Poland was home to very poor farmers. Cultivated soil was limited, and most of the territory was swamps. The hostile climate was also not helpful, and these farmers lived on meager productions of wheat, corn, potatoes, and a few vegetables and some animals.

Finally we found and entered the house, which consisted of one room. In the center of this room stood a brick hearth used for heating as well as cooking. The house was furnished with a primitive wooden table and benches. The dim light of an oil lamp gave the impression of a fairy tale. It felt gloriously warm. The farmer's wife welcomed us and gave us a place to sit. I was handed a knife and was asked to peel potatoes. This process was completely new to me. I didn't know how to handle a long, sharp knife, much less how to peel potatoes. The truth is, Mother was not much better, but we did the best we could. We were instructed to make the peelings very thin so as not to waste potatoes. My stomach growled in anticipation of a hot meal. Boiled potatoes and a plain piece of bread looked like a feast to me.

After eating, we were shown to a corner of the room with straw on the floor, which would be our bed for the night. The minute my head reached the floor, I fell asleep.

We were shaken awake before sunrise by a woman's voice whispering, "Soviet patrol in the village. They're coming here. If you're found you'll be taken back and punished."

Quickly we jumped into the cellar and hid in a darkened corner. I heard voices speaking in an unknown language—it was Russian. A woman's voice in Polish said, "Nobody's here. Nobody's here."

We heard the sound of heavy boots walking around the room above us. Suddenly the cellar cover was opened and somebody looked in. We were not seen and the cover was closed once again. When we climbed back up from the cellar, my mother discovered that her wedding band was missing from her finger. To her, this was a bad omen. The only possible place to look for it was on the straw bed. She would not give up and started to search, removing straw by straw. We had limited time, since we had to move fast out of the village before the next Russian patrol. Stubbornly she continued searching, ignoring pleas to abandon her search and leave. At almost the last minute, her efforts were rewarded. She found her wedding ring and her spirits were restored.

After breakfast of leftover potatoes and a little bread, we left the house. A cart pulled by a horse was already outside and we accommodated ourselves in it, covering our heads with scarves borrowed from the farmer, native style. It simulated two natives on the cart, which was quite a common sight. We were heading toward a railroad station a few hours down the road.

We arrived at the town of Zaremby Koscielne. The mission of the smugglers was accomplished, and we were left in the railroad station. The station was packed with people of mixed origins, so we blended in very well inside this Poland occupied by Russia. Soviet patrols were everywhere, but now we were just two of many wanderers. With difficulty, Mother was able to buy two tickets that would take us to Białystok. I don't remember how long we had to wait for the train, or how long the trip itself was. Once inside the train car, time was of no importance. The only thing that mattered was that at last we were safe and on our way to join Kazik and Father.

Early in the morning of the next day, we arrived in Białystok. Once in the city, we mixed easily with the rest of the population. Białystok was a textile city similar to Łódź but smaller, with a substantial Jewish population. It was not difficult to find the Ravins' apartment. I remember a woman opening the door for us. The minute we introduced ourselves, her eyes opened in bewilderment. She asked us in and said, "I have a surprise for you." Then she disappeared into the next room. We heard her say, "Wake up. Somebody is waiting for you. Hurry."

Soon Kazik was standing in the door looking at us. For a few seconds, none of us could move. We just stood there looking at each other. Then we threw ourselves in each other's arms, crying. After so many agonizing months, we were together again. We started talking at the same time, asking questions. Our words flowed faster than we could express them. We wanted to know everything at once, and were laughing and crying at the same time.

The absence of Father surprised us, but Kazik told us he'd found work in the city of Orsha, U.S.S.R. and had started the procedure to obtain permission and the necessary documents to bring his family. Kazik had stayed with the Ravins, and they were kind enough also to provide Mother and me with shelter and some of the precious food that was so hard to find.

At last, we were able to take a shower and remove our incredibly dirty clothing. We borrowed garments, ate, and looked forward to sleep in real beds.

We talked for long hours. We learned of Kazik and Father's journey. When they left us, they had started walking as quickly as possible from Łódź to Warsaw, about eighty kilometers away, passing a great exodus of people heading in the same direction. They had no luggage with them in contrast to others, so they were able to walk faster. They saw destruction everywhere. Entire deserted villages lay in ruins. At noon they reached a small farm and they stopped for a drink. At the first hut, the farmers had nothing to offer them so they entered a second hut a few meters away in which some milk was available. Not having food since that morning, milk was wonderful to them.

No sooner did they start to drink than airplanes appeared and bombed the farm. Terrible explosions and fires could be seen. Huts were reduced to nothing but rubble and smoke as a rain of bullets and shrapnel fell from the passing planes. Kazik and Father threw themselves to the ground in a ditch and when they ventured out after the raid, all that they saw was smoke, dust, and fire. The huts, people, cattle—the entire farm—was gone. How they avoided death is a mystery.

They walked all the way to Warsaw, barely ahead of the German tanks, stopping only for short rests and sleeping on the grass or in forests, their feet covered with blisters. Kazik, not used to this kind of hardship, almost had to be carried by Father. They traveled the eighty kilometers in twenty-eight hours. This was the only way for them to escape. They reached our cousin's apartment in Warsaw, where they finally rested and healed their sore feet.

Then the siege of Warsaw started. The building in which Kazik and Father stayed was hit. Walls fell. Fire and broken glass were everywhere. Dust covered everything. Luckily they were unscathed and managed to emerge through the rubble. They fled the burning street. The whole city was on fire by then. Almost every building was destroyed. Food was impossible to obtain. People helped each other, sharing hot water to drink and whatever scanty food that had been abandoned. This continued for days; then, one morning, the air raids stopped and an uneasy silence embraced the city. After a valiant defense by the Polish army, Warsaw fell and the Germans entered its suburbs.

The only way Kazik and Father could survive was to continue east. Some of their friends, in spite of Father's pleas to come along, stayed behind. In the last minutes, Kazik and Father managed to sneak through German lines and continue walking to the Soviet zone. They walked for days, spending nights in whatever places were available and surviving on bread they obtained in villages along the way. After crossing the River Bug, they were able to find a train. Transformed into dirty, exiled, homeless vagabonds, they reached Białystok and shelter in the Ravins' home.

When Father arrived in Białystok, he desperately looked for some way to earn money. Soon he realized the danger he was in. Being very active and well known in Bund, he (along with every other Bundist) was an enemy of Communism. This membership was a Soviet crime punishable by forced labor in Siberia or incarceration in the gulag. Father was in danger if he was recognized. Any Polish Communist might turn him in. This possibility put the whole Ravin family in jeopardy, especially since Mr. Ravin was a Bundist himself.

This weighed heavily on his mind, so Father did a daring thing. He registered for work inside Russia. Some days later, he was accepted and handed a number to present to the commandant for departure. The Ravins begged Father not to go, fearing disaster. Father, on the other hand, begged the Ravins to go to Russia with him and take their chances. They were too afraid to go and decided to stay. Thus they missed this chance of surviving. All the family died in a concentration camp when Germany occupied Białystok and the rest of Poland in 1941.

Finally, Father was sent to a factory in Orsha, Byelorussia, where he started working as a bookkeeper, passing as a simple working man liberated from Polish capitalism by socialism in the U.S.S.R. He also had another big secret which, if exposed, would be deadly: He had a mother, brothers, and sisters living in Moscow with whom he had no contact since the Communist Revolution. He had escaped from Russia during the early years of the socialist movement. In Russia, to have any contact with the outside world was forbidden, so he'd had no communication with his relatives in years. He took a big gamble venturing a return to Russia.

With great difficulty, we were able to communicate with Father and let him know of our arrival in Białystok. We stayed in the Ravins' home for some weeks, awaiting permission to go to Orsha to join Father. The Ravins' apartment was not big, but they made room for anyone who needed refuge. Food was shared. All of us helped with the housework as much as we could. Later on, one room was confiscated by the Soviet government for the use of an officer and his family. This already crowded apartment became even more so. The kitchen and one bathroom were shared by everyone. For us, this was something new. For Soviet citizens, it was the normal way of living.

In order to enter Byelorussia, a work permit was required. The Soviet agency had to request a person for a specific type of work. Since Mother's profession was teaching, it was relatively easy for Father to obtain the necessary documents. We children, Kazik and myself, were automatically included.

As soon as we obtained the affidavit, we were ready for departure. We did not have too much luggage, only a few garments given to us by the Jewish community. Mother was advised to buy a little oil stove, which later on proved to be a treasure and a blessing. And so with tearful goodbyes, we bid farewell to the Ravins and left Białystok to go into an unknown country that was a Communist region.

We had to wait hours for the train because there was no schedule for departures. The station was crowded with people, and we had to watch constantly to be sure we would not miss our train. We stood on an open platform in bitter cold. When the train finally arrived, the entire mob ran for boarding. The three of us held together in fear of being separated, pushing ourselves to the first available boxcar, which was already filled with people. We were happy to be in. There was just standing room.

The usual time from Białystok to Vitebsk (now Vitsyebsk), the first station on the soil of Soviet Russia, was only two hours. It took us six. There we transferred to another train, which consisted of boxcars with no benches and which was already crowded to capacity. We managed to squeeze ourselves inside. Finding a small place in the corner of the boxcar, we occupied it as fast as we could. Doing so, we were able to continue our trip sitting, which took us a few days. On the way, wherever the train would stop, everyone ran out, including us, in search of something to eat. Usually we were able to obtain some bread, occasionally some milk, from the villages.

At one point I found a small insect crawling on my arm. I showed it to Mother. "Look," I said. Mother took one look at it, and her face turned white. She shook my arm, causing the insect to fall on the floor, and she stepped on it. It was one of the fearful lice, which were notorious for causing typhus. We had truly entered the Communist paradise.

We arrived in Orsha late at night, tired, dirty, and looking like beggars. Father was aroused from his sleep by a Soviet authority, the administrator of the building, who informed Father that he'd received a cable with news of our arrival. He jumped out of bed and ran to the railroad station. After so many months of being apart—months of horror and destruction, months of suffering and misery, months of despair and hopelessness—in the darkness of that night my family fell into each other's arms, not ashamed of the tears rolling down our cheeks, not able to produce a word or even a sound, just standing there, holding close together, not feeling the cold or seeing people around us. In this precious and short moment, the past was forgotten and the present was sweet and wonderful. We were together again.

The spell was broken by an official who ordered us to leave the premises at once. Unauthorized persons were forbidden to linger upon arrival. Indeed, the station seemed otherwise deserted.

We went to Father's quarters, a room that he shared with six other people. Each of them had a bed, and in the center was a table and a few chairs. Kazik and I found sleeping space on the floor. I fell asleep immediately to the gentle whispers of Mother and Father. And so began a new phase of my life as a citizen of the Soviet Union.

It was difficult in Orsha, as it was in the rest of Russia, to obtain any kind of accommodation because of the shortage of housing. The procedure to obtain accommodations was very complicated, long, and bureaucratic. We learned of a room, vacant at the moment. The previous occupant had been promoted and moved to better quarters. Father had a good relationship with the factory director, and he helped us with the permit to move. It was an extraordinary accomplishment. The building to which we moved was a four-story complex on the last row at the edge of town, facing the railroad. The apartment consisted of three rooms. In one of them lived four young single women, friendly and sympathetic to us. One of the girls had acute tuberculosis, and I remember her coughing pitifully during the night. In the other room lived a family who was not pleased to have us as neighbors because they themselves had wanted our room.

The doors to all rooms opened into a small hall. In the hall was one small toilet for us all and a room to be used by everyone as a kitchen. This type of living was typical in the U.S.S.R.—one room for an entire family.

This is when our little one-burner oil stove became our greatest treasure. It was the only way to cook. Each family had its own, and it was forbidden to touch anyone else's. Many unpleasant situations emerged because of this rule.

The other problem was the toilet shared by twelve people, especially in the morning, when there was a rush to go to work and school. To clean the toilet, hall, and kitchen, we rotated every week. This is when I learned to scrub the floor and (what I hated the most) to clean the toilet, which, after so intensive and not so careful use, was quite dirty. At that point, Mother was in no condition to do such work and I was grown up enough to help.

Hanna and her mother in March 1941, in Orsha, Byelorussia. In this room, where the family lived, was an armoire with a mirror—a real treasure—a bed for Hanna's parents, a table with two chairs, a sofa on which Kazik slept, and a small cot for Hanna.

Mother started working as a technical drawing teacher, which was a required subject preparing students for future technical education. Kazik worked in the technical division of the factory where Father was a bookkeeper and I was enrolled in school.

Our settlement was on the outskirts of the town in which a big factory was located, along with rows of red apartment houses for the workers. There was a general store, a hospital or clinic, a meeting hall, and the school.

Soon after our arrival, I started school. I walked to this strange school for the first time on a cold, wintry morning, alone and with a heavy heart. Other children of all ages walked in groups, laughing and talking. The minute they spotted me, they pointed fingers in my direction. *"Polachka!"* they said to me. This was a derogatory term for a Polish person. Apparently a foreigner such as myself had not been seen by them before. They approached me and touched me, to assure themselves I was real, and said things to me that I could not understand. With tears in my eyes, I thought of my friends left behind. I understood that I had escaped the danger of immediate death, but I could not understand the meaninglessness of my supposed sanctuary. I was scared of these children, of these unknown buildings, classrooms, teachers, and language.

I let everyone pass me as I slowly approached the school. Once inside, I was directed to the principal's office. He asked me some questions, which I could not understand, but he knew who I was. He escorted me to my room, explaining something to the teacher, and left. I stood in front of the class confused and terrified as all eyes focused on me, and then I realized that the teacher was introducing me to the class. Finally, to my relief, he pointed to a desk, which I understood he was assigning to me. I sat down and pretended to be invisible. I was handed books, papers, and pencils.

As the day progressed, my situation was not any better. I was unable to communicate with anyone and was constantly touched and laughed at. They, too, could not understand why I did not answer as they talked to me, taking me for hearing impaired. At one of the recesses, I ran to use the outhouse, which I needed very badly. I could not believe my eyes when I found it. The one room had a long board with rows of holes, one next to the other. Without ceremony, girls were using them standing up. I was terribly embarrassed and confused, but I had to use it.

At the end of that first school day, when at last I reached our room, I lay down on the bed and cried uncontrollably. The next day I refused to go to school. To comfort me, my parents talked to me after assuring ourselves that the neighbors had left for work. In a Communist regime, even the walls can hear. In low voices, my parents spoke to me.

"We took a big chance to come here, choosing the lesser of two dangerous situations," Father said. "We escaped death from the Nazis, and for this we have to be thankful. But we are not completely safe here. From now on you have to remember that in Poland you were the daughter of two hard-working people, that you went to public school, and that you lived in a small apartment. You must pretend to be happy to be liberated from capitalism by the Soviets. Never speak about the business we had or the reunions in our house. All our lives depend on this. If it is discovered who we were, we will be declared enemies of the revolution and arrested. From now on, it is your job to remember everything about our new identities."

"You must go to school," Mother said then, "since not sending a child to school is punishable. It is difficult, but it has to be done."

So I got ready and went to school, remembering well what I had been told. I presumed that in order to save our lives it was okay not to tell the truth, or rather to avoid answering questions when possible.

Little by little, with help from my parents, who both spoke Russian perfectly, I learned the Russian alphabet and language. At that time we were forbidden to speak Polish, so there could be no secret talk among us, and we were forced to use only Russian.

In the Communist educational system, our principal subject was Marxism-Leninism. Other subjects such as mathematics and geography took second place. There was a Russian name attributed to each and every scientific discovery. Mathematics, physics, chemical laws, and history were completely changed to suit Communist Russian doctrine. Without passing Marxism-Leninism, one was not promoted to the next year. I learned how fat capitalists oppress the poor working class, that religion is the opium of the proletariat used to subdue people and distract their minds, and that God did not exist.

"Pray to God," we were told, "and ask God to give you some candy." I did pray, with all my heart. I wouldn't mind having some candy. Needless to say, there was no candy. "And now," the teacher said, "ask our beloved Stalin for some candy." As we did so, candy appeared and was given to us. It tasted so sweet and delicious.

This simplistic method was extremely effective. All concept of God known to me collapsed. I did not have answers to my own questions.

Our lives were very structured. Young children, until the second grade, belonged to a group called Oktyabr (Octobrists), for the October revolution. From third grade up, children formed a group called Pioniers (Young Pioneers). We had to wear red scarves rolled like a tie, with a ring that had Soviet emblems holding the ends together. I was the only one in school who did not have a red scarf. In due time, and without a choice, I was honored by being admitted to the Young Pioneers. In a big assembly of the entire school, and with lots of festivity, all the third graders were gathered to be introduced and congratulated on this big event of their lives. The only older girl to be admitted to the Young Pioneers was me. I felt terribly out of place, the only big girl surrounded by little third graders. With my eyes looking down, I stood last in line. Since everybody was happy and proud to be there, I had to force a smile on my face. When endless speeches, singing, and congratulations were over, I was glad to be back in my class.

I learned well and faithfully answered questions, passing the required tests. I could not help but wonder in silence, however. What bothered me most was why, if we are not responsible for our parents' actions, we were constantly asked about our parents, grandparents, aunts, and uncles. We were required to fill pages and pages of questionnaires about our relatives, their affiliations, professions, conduct, and addresses. If one member of the family was presumed guilty, the whole family was punished and arrested. This situation presented a big problem for us, since Father's family lived in Moscow.

4
LIVING BY RUSSIAN RULES

After World War I, Father's parents, along with his brothers and sisters, emigrated to Moscow from Vitebsk (now Vitsyebsk). When his brother George was drafted, Father had presented himself in his brother's place because he was just recovering from typhoid fever and therefore knew he'd be immediately dismissed, which he was. Uncle George fled the country and established himself in Sweden first, then in the United States. Father was already an active member of Bund, and so he was forced to leave Russia, escaping to Poland. He settled in Łódź, met and married my mother, and established his business and his family. Since Father's political actions were punishable in Russia, all contact with my grandparents, aunts, and uncles was cut off. Officially, for the benefit of the family, it was declared that their sons were presumed dead.

I knew about the existence of this family but had never even seen their pictures. Father longed to see his mother and sisters and brothers again. His father had already died. The problem was, how to execute this project without putting everyone's life in jeopardy?

Communication with the outside world was forbidden in Russia. However, there was a regular mail system established within the country. From Orsha, Father mailed a letter to his sister Fania, who lived with her husband Marc and her mother, my grandmother Raquel. Father had concealed his true identity, and when Fania received the letter, she panicked. However, when she realized who it was from, everyone, especially Grandmother, was overjoyed to have news from him. An elaborate plan was constructed.

First my Uncle David would make the trip to Orsha. With some difficulty he obtained permission to travel, which was not easy because without *komandirovka* (permission), one was not allowed to travel. Uncle David arrived in Orsha in the evening, and he and

Father met at the station. After many years of being separated, they had to be careful not to draw any attention to themselves. They stayed in the waiting room all night and talked, but they had to be very careful to conceal their emotions. In the morning, Uncle David took the train back to Moscow. The same procedure was used with Fania. They too stayed all night at the station, talking, and by sunrise, she took another train back to Moscow. Father went to work and when asked where he'd been in the evening, he answered, "I visited with some friends."

The time came when my grandmother could wait no longer to see her son. We began to arrange for her visit. Somehow Father was able to find an old sofa and transport it to our living quarters. By now, we were fully furnished with two beds, a sofa with a table in front of it and three chairs, and a small space for storage and to hang our few belongings. Father would sleep with Kazik, I with Mother, and Grandmother was to have the sofa. We informed our neighbors that some lost distant relative would come to see us, and this was accepted.

Finally Grandmother Raquel came. I remember being overcome by emotion. I wanted to be with her very much. But she was a stranger to me and I to her. She did not know Mother or Kazik or me, and a few hours is not enough time to become close. She was a very religious woman in spite of the prohibitions. She prayed three times a day in Hebrew and obeyed the dietary laws. In our case, it was very easy, since food was limited and we did not have meat. How difficult it must have been for her, not having seen her son since his youth and not having any contact with him at all, and how joyful it must have been to be finally reunited with him—with the bonus of a daughter-in-law and two grandchildren. Her time with us was very short, however, and soon she had to leave. After she left, we enjoyed remembering her visit and feasting on some sugar she had brought to us from Moscow.

We entered a routine of everyday living and struggled to keep our minds on the right path demanded by the socialist regime. Any slip of the tongue could bring disaster. Food and clothing were very difficult to obtain, as were shoes, soap, and any kind of everyday necessity. Long lines on the street in front of the store indicated that some product had arrived and was going to be sold. There was no question asked about what kind of product, as long as something, anything, was available. The word for this was *dayut*, meaning "is given," in spite of the fact that we had to pay for whatever there was. Since we were absolutely in need of everything, we stayed in these lines, sometimes for hours and hours.

I became a specialist at sneaking in lines and often ran very early to secure a place. Bread was the first necessity, and it was very important to be on time to obtain it. After standing for a long time on cold, windy days, we were lucky if the store even opened. Bread would disappear quickly from the shelves, and once it was gone, the store would close until the next shipment. The unlucky ones who did not get there on time had to go home empty handed.

Many times I stood hungry and cold, wondering if the store would have something. Sometimes there was nothing available; other times, the goods came. Once, when I finally entered the store, I found that underwear was on sale. It was all the same lilac color in three sizes, and only three pair per person were permitted. We needed these very badly, so size was of no importance. I was growing up and my garments were too small for me. Sometimes we got bars of soap, and one time we were able to get some dried soup.

There was a big commotion one day when the word spread that shoes were going to be "given." Again, all the shoes were the same, one style for men and another style for women, in big, medium, or small. I learned not to be choosy.

One of the most important and most difficult things to obtain was oil for our little stove. Without oil, there was never any hot water or any kind of cooking possible. Eating raw potatoes is not pleasant. Needless to say, these lines were enormous. It was not unusual to be in a fight for a place in line.

We were constantly bombarded in school about how wonderful Communism was. Everyone is equal, they told us. So, I wondered, if everyone is equal, where do the important Communist Party members stand in line? Why do they have shoes and warm coats? Why do they have better living facilities? To my understanding, there was no equality.

Unbelievably, we got a letter from Marie, who was living in the Warsaw ghetto. She told us they were starving. At that time, for propaganda reasons, to demonstrate the abundance of food in the

U.S.S.R., Polish refugees were permitted to send one package to relatives. So we made a package of our pea soup and bars of soap and sent it to Marie through the International Red Cross. We had no way in which to seal these items and no proper paper to cover them.

I went with Father to take the package to the headquarters of the Red Cross in Orsha. The official there gave it one look and said, "It is not packed properly."

"But it is packed according to the instructions on my previous visit here," Father answered, to no avail. We walked back home and added the requested packaging, which was a wooden box, sealed and labeled. He took it again to the Red Cross. This time, it was requested that the entire box should be covered with burlap material. Arguing was useless, so he walked back home to find the required material. After searching, pleading, and a proper bribe, we found a necessary piece. We covered the entire box, then wrote Marie's address with ink, which was also not easy to obtain. The next time Father returned, the Red Cross official was surprised, but the package was accepted. From our house to Orsha was a six-kilometer walk both ways. Father had to cover this distance three times, eighteen kilometers in all, to mail this package.

We got a letter from Marie three months later. She did receive the package, but unfortunately the penetrating smell of the very poor-quality soap had invaded the powdered soup, which was not very tasty to start with. Nevertheless, Marie stretched the contents of the soup, diluting it with water and onions. This was the last contact we had with Marie.

Once, Mother was commissioned to create a painting. She was given canvas and oil and immediately went to work with great enthusiasm, happy once again to have a brush in her hands. She worked hard creating a patriotic scene: A Soviet soldier with a handsome, smiling face stood in a magnificent uniform holding a red flag with Communist emblems. She painted an incredibly beautiful background with light and colors, which was her particular expertise, bringing the canvas to life. This painting was a beautiful piece of Communist propaganda. Proudly she presented the finished picture to the principal. He looked at it and his face turned pale with terror. He covered the picture at once with paper, thrust it at Mother, and ordered her to destroy it. "I did not ask you to create a masterpiece," he said. "This painting is not approved by a party official and thus we cannot accept it. You should copy what the Communist party assigned you to do and not use your imagination." Sadly, this was the last time she was permitted to paint, and losing her work took away her spirit. She was an artist, and without her art, she was lost. However, she was permitted to continue teaching technical graphics according to the books she was given as guidance. Independence and initiative were not permitted. Soviet citizens had to follow the Communist party line, which dictated every aspect of life.

I, too, learned hard lessons. In my Russian language class, we were given an essay to write about Moscow. I wrote an excellent composition, using as many Communist slogans as possible. I outdid myself in patriotism and devotion to the country and Stalinism. I used lines from songs about Moscow. It sounded terrific, even if I did not use my own thoughts. The teacher was well impressed. "Did anybody help you to write?" he asked.

"No," I replied. "I did this myself."

"There are no errors in grammar or spelling," he said. "This is a job well done. But I cannot give you an A. You came from a capitalist country, so you cannot be better than our children here. Be glad that I'll give you a B." I stood there, humiliated and laughed at.

I had been taught that discrimination did not exist, but here at school it was discovered that I was Jewish and I was discriminated against. Being a combination of Polish and Jewish was the worst combination in one person's identity. I was *polachka,* a foreigner, capitalist, oppressor of the working class, and a Jew. This last was somewhat confusing to my classmates, however, because their knowledge of Jews was not clear. According to my classmates, I should have a big, runny nose, black hair, myopic eyes, and heavy glasses. I was constantly asked why I did not fit into these categories, and I had no answer. It was decided among my peers that something was wrong with me, even though my accomplishments in sports were more than average, which had great value in Russia. Consequently, two of my Jewish classmates also rejected me. More than once I came home crying.

In the U.S.S.R., the work week was composed of five working days and one day off. There were no religious holidays, and Saturday and Sunday were like any other days. The only holidays we had were days of national celebration. The biggest of these was the celebration of the October Revolution. If this holiday fell on a working day, it was moved to the day that corresponded to the day off. As a result, there were always five days of work. We had two school breaks, one of them being the winter vacation, another the summer vacation.

Since Christmas did not exist but there was need of some kind of festivity, New Year's Day was selected as a holiday. In time, the Christmas tree was substituted for the New Year's tree. Toward the end of the year, preparations for the upcoming year started. It was announced that the school would be allowed to have a tree and a party to welcome the New Year on December 31. Vibrations of excitement were felt throughout the school. At once, all students in Mother's class, under her direction and with her help, started preparing decorations for the tree. We were handed red papers from which we cut Soviet red flags and red stars with Soviet emblems in the middle. We made red paper strips with Communist slogans written on them. With these things, we decorated our New Year's tree.

The completed scene was almost unbelievable. The traditional Christmas tree was transformed into a tree of glory to Socialism, love for our great Father Stalin, and devotion to the Communist regime. With the rest of the students, I sang patriotic songs that had nothing to do with the coming New Year. We recited assigned slogans and thanked our beloved Stalin. I couldn't figure out what we were thanking him for. Perhaps it was for the one candy we were allowed to have and a slice of some kind of bread, which was supposed to be a piece of cake. This food was given to us by Dedushka Moroz (Grandfather Frost), who wore a red soldier's uniform, a red hat, and a white beard and mustache. Santa Claus was forbidden and did not exist in the U.S.S.R. Instead we were fed with propaganda and demonstrations of the goodness of Soviet soldiers. We were also led in traditional Russian dances. Our New Year's party ended with our principal's speech, more Communist slogans, and wishing each other a happy Soviet New Year.

5
OUTRUNNING THE GERMANS

The year 1941 started and apparently there were no changes in Russian-German relations. The information about the war in Europe was very limited, and what there was praised Germany for her victories. The only news we could listen to was on our one-station radio, which also transmitted approved music during a few hours each day. This radio could be heard from every room and every apartment, since everyone had the same radio or, rather, speaker. Very little was mentioned about the ghettoes in Poland or the destruction and persecution of Jews. We could only wonder about the terrible suffering and the destiny of those we left behind.

During the months that followed, however, Father had convictions that the pact with Germany was coming to an end and that war was inevitable. Therefore, we started to consider our options for the future. Orsha would be the first on the front lines of fire. Russian technology and equipment were no match for the German army.

Mother had an aunt who lived in Gor'kiy (now Nizhniy Novgorod), which was an industrial city. This location seemed to be a good place to move. Father started to work for the possibility of transferring there. He had become a friend of his factory's director, who liked and appreciated my father and many times sought his advice. After some talk, the director found no objection to commissioning Father to a factory in Gor'kiy.

We found Aunt Gucia's address and sent her a short note. She was my maternal grandfather's sister and was the widow of a wealthy Russian industrialist. After the revolution, she was left with two daughters in the house that used to be hers but now belonged to the government. She still lived in this house, presently sharing it with one of her daughters and her family, as well as with others.

Father obtained the proper permission to travel and left for Gor'kiy. He visited a tearful Aunt Gucia, who had not seen her family in Poland for many years. Her daughter's husband, however, was a member of the Communist Party, and she was afraid he would denounce any stranger in the house. With difficulty, Father was able to obtain work in a factory in Gor'kiy and was to be transferred there as a highly qualified and necessary worker.

When he returned to us, it was decided that we would move sometime in the summer after the end of the school year, so Mother would be able to come, too. For all of us, this meant lots of documents, permissions, transfers, and questionnaires to fill out, to satisfy the Soviet bureaucracy. We had to go from one official to another to obtain these documents. In Russia, nothing would progress except *po blatu* (by influence), in other words, with a bribe of some kind to the right person. This required the assistance of some friend, who "knew the right person." The director of the Orsha factory was instrumental in this endeavor. With high hopes of moving further east away from the German hordes, we continued our daily routines.

One day, a party commissar, Comrade Semiaszko, proposed to Father that he perform a so-called social mission as the best qualified worker. Because of Father's accurate and quick bookkeeping, the Party awarded him with this voluntary assignment. We all were excited. This meant Father was in good standing with the officials.

A few days later, however, Father came home terribly upset and shaken. On this day, Comrade Semiaszko had summoned Father to his office and asked if he had a business of his own in Poland and if he was a Bund member. Father was struck with fear but managed to answer with surprise on his face. "Comrade Semiaszko, I told you that I was a bookkeeper and never a Bund member. I would not be here otherwise."

Luckily for us, Comrade Semiaszko was fond of Father and accepted this answer. We found out later that one of the women informers working for the NKVD, which later became the KGB, had denounced Father to Comrade Semiaszko.

We were safe for the moment but feared that the NKVD would dig into our past. For us, as well as for our entire family in Moscow, this exposure would mean arrest and forced labor in Siberia. Even

Father's eternal optimism abandoned him this time. So many people dear to him were exposed to the possibility of death, and he could do nothing to prevent it.

The summer of 1941 was approaching. I was happy when school ended and I could be at home. The weather turned warm and pleasant. Trees grew new leaves, grass between buildings was green again, and flowers started to bloom. We put away our heavy clothing and our skis. Children, enclosed for such long months inside walls, were free at last to pour outside—playing, running, laughing at the fresh early summer month caressed by the warm sun. We frequently sat in the sun reading, or walking and picking flowers, especially the lovely sunflowers. These flowers, when mature, had delicious seeds which were wonderful to crack between our teeth and then to chew the sweet soft inside.

On special occasions we were organized into gymnastic groups at the sports center in school, with a coach training us on the gym equipment. I loved these exercises and was quite good at them. I had dreams that one day I would be a great figure skater on ice and felt gymnastics was good for my development toward this goal.

Then one day Mother did not come home. She was always home before Father. When he arrived and she was not there, he asked us where she was. Neither Kazik nor I had paid any attention to her absence. When she did not come home after an hour, we started to worry and knew that something must be wrong. As the evening progressed, we panicked. We could not find her anywhere. There was no point in inquiring about her at the police quarters or the NKVD, since they would not give out any information. The only thing we could do was to wait and pray for her.

At nightfall, we saw her coming in the distance. We all ran to her, hardly believing we were seeing her again. She was shaking, very pale, and almost collapsed in Father's arms. We all grabbed her and helped her home, pretending that she walked on her own so nothing would look suspicious to the neighbors. After she recovered and regained her strength, we learned what had happened.

In the afternoon, as she enjoyed the beautiful summer weather, she took paper and pencil and sat down in front of the railroad to draw. A man passed by and noticed what she was doing and requested to be shown her passport. Since she was just outside the house, she didn't have it with her. She offered to go upstairs to get it and told him he was welcome to come with her. Instead, he took her to the NKVD. There an NKVD superior officer questioned her. "We know who you are," he said. "Your husband is a capitalist, a member of the Bund counterrevolutionists."

She was led to a cell, where she was requested to write a biography of both herself and father. They threatened that if she were not truthful, she would not see the next daylight. After an hour, an officer removed her work and took her to another cell. The same procedure was repeated twice. She desperately tried to remember exactly what she had written before, so as not to be caught in making any small mistake.

Finally they led her upstairs to the commissar's office. Three other agents were there, studying her writings. Pretending to be calm, she started to look straight into the commissar's face. Surprised by this behavior, the commissar asked her why she was looking at him. "You have a very interesting face," she answered. "I wish I could paint you."

She was released for the time being and was allowed to go home. Days later, our friend, also a refugee from Poland, told us that he, as a person who was trusted, was called to the NKVD and asked about our family. He told them this denunciation was absurd and said it was a proven fact that Mother was a teacher and had accepted Soviet citizenship voluntarily. This explanation was acceptable for the time being, but we knew it was a matter of time before we were exposed and arrested.

A week later, on Sunday, June 22, without warning the first German bomb fell. Only after the first air raid did the radio broadcast the news of German attacks on the U.S.S.R., breaking the pact of nonaggression. Once again, we were in the middle of war. With the chaos that followed the outbreak of the war, we were saved from our problems with the NKVD.

Living through bombardments once is enough for a lifetime. Going through air raids for the second time was more than I could take. Our present building had no basement, and there was no shelter at all. Also, the warning sirens didn't work, which greatly hindered the anti-aircraft machine guns that were supposed to prevent attacks by German airplanes. In spite of the radio news telling us about the victory of the Soviet army and of the heavy German casualties, German tanks were approaching and air raids were continuous. Bombs hit part of the factory and explosions were heard everywhere.

During the night we stood on the first-floor staircase, which was the only protection we could find. One of the bombs hit the edge of our house, and another hit the railroad out back. I heard cracking walls and was covered by glass and dust before darkness overcame me. I woke up in Mother's arms. She was yelling for water, which was impossible to obtain. I heard Father's anxious voice: "Is she all right?" Fortunately, no one was hurt, and I quickly recovered from fainting. By Monday morning, it was obvious that the Germans had found no resistance and were advancing.

Tuesday the situation got worse. In desperation, Father approached the factory director, asking for permission to go further east and advised him to do the same. To fall into German hands meant instant death for all of us. There was no time to waste.

After the director and a party official held a brief conference, evacuation of high-ranking personnel's wives and children started. Somehow, Father realized that we would be left on our own. He ran home to tell us and in a matter of minutes, we had two backpacks ready, one for Father and Kazik, the other for Mother and me. We found a truck parked in front of the factory building, which was filled with Communist leaders' children and wives. Father threw me inside, but they refused to let Mother in and pushed her aside. Father fought back and by force put her on the truck. He threw in one of the backpacks and quietly told her that he and Kazik would start walking toward a kolkhoz, a communal farm, which was twenty kilometers east of Orsha. At one point, young men were ordered to go back to Orsha to work on the defense. Kazik was among them.

By nightfall Father reached the kolkhoz. We had arrived earlier and were relieved to see him, but were shattered by fear for Kazik. When we were settled for the evening in the kolkhoz meeting place, Father told us he'd handed us the wrong backpack, so Mother and I had no change of clothing. He had realized his mistake shortly after our departure, but, not knowing if he would be able to join us, he took our clothes out.

The next day Father was stricken by terrible pain. He had a strangulated hernia, and the only doctor to be found was on the front line of battle. Without help, Father would die. He was given a cart pulled by a horse, and Mother took him to seek a doctor. I was left alone with the rest of the refugees. Our group consisted of about two hundred people, mostly people who joined us in the kolkhoz from our factory. We were led by Comrade Bobovnikov, who was in charge of evacuation to Vyaz´ma, four hundred kilometers east.

I watched as Father lay on the bottom of the cart that was pulling my parents away from me toward the firing line. Mother walked on the side, holding his hand in desperation and sorrow, torn between Father's illness and leaving me behind with strangers. She had no choice, though. I waited until they disappeared from view, tears rolling down my cheeks. I heard women talking, saying "orphan," as they approached to take me inside. I sat in the corner on the floor where we slept. More than death, I feared being left alone without my parents.

I was with other refugees now, and they consoled me and took me under their wings. A woman came with one egg and sat beside me. "I was able to find this egg," she said. "This is for you. Eat it." How she obtained an egg where only dry food was rationed was a mystery to me then, and is still so today. She was a mother, too, and wanted to calm me down. There was no cooking facility. She simply punched the egg on both sides and handed it to me. I drank the egg between sobbing and savoring this delicacy which I'd almost forgotten.

At dusk, I heard yelling: "They're coming back!" They did come back, and they were unharmed. At the battlefield hospital, they found a doctor who was able to reduce Father's hernia, saving his life, until a more favorable time for surgery. I had my parents back!

In spite of official communiques telling of Soviet victories and German retreats, the real news from the front was bad. The German army was advancing at an alarming speed.

On our third day in the kolkhoz, it was announced that horse-drawn wagons were being sent from Orsha and that early the next morning we would move on. Children would ride in the wagons, but anyone able to walk would do so. We faced an agonizing decision, since we didn't know the fate of Kazik. We couldn't stay behind, however, since it was only a matter of time until the Germans occupied this kolkhoz. We forced ourselves to leave without Kazik.

At sunrise, the camp was ready. Time was crucial for survival. As the wagons started moving and people started walking, we saw someone running toward us. Incredibly, it was Kazik with one of his friends. If he had been delayed in coming another ten minutes, we would have been gone, lost to each other perhaps forever. At that moment, nothing mattered except that we were together again.

When Kazik was sent back to Orsha, he was assigned to build bunkers with other young men. At one point, the factory director spotted him, handed him a loaf of bread, and told him to leave and run as fast as he could to the kolkhoz where we stayed. Because of him, Kazik was able to live.

Our group of nine wagons made slow progress through the villages and kolkhozes on the dusty country roads. We stopped only for short rests and food, some dry goods, and rice cooked over campfires. In the town of Dubrova, our leader, Bobovnikov, found some sacks of black hardtack (unleavened bread made in very hard, large rounds) which renewed our supplies. After short sleeps, we moved again so we could escape from the approaching Germans as quickly as possible. With the passage of hours, our group became smaller, because some refugee families felt no need of escaping the Germans and decided to go back. I think secretly they may have been glad of the German occupation. Not belonging to the Communist party, they felt they had no reason to fear Germans.

After three days of wandering on roads far from civilization, we reached one kolkhoz where we stopped for a longer rest. Orders reached us there, however, that requested all men to register for the army in the kolkhoz of Lida, not too far away. There was nothing we could do but once again say goodbye as Kazik and Father jumped into waiting trucks. Women and children stayed behind. We would continue our march on our own, tending the horses. This time there was no crying, just a terrible sadness surrounding all of us.

After the truck with the men advanced a few kilometers, it was stopped by a group of men marching from Orsha. Comrade Semiaszko was with them. Recognizing Father, he approached us and appealed to him to return to the women because Orsha had already fallen into German hands and the Germans were advancing rapidly. He, as a party leader, had to go to Smolensk to join the army. He pleaded with Father to take his wife and two young children to safety, reminding him that in Orsha he had saved Father from the NKVD.

So once again we were reunited, but the rest of the women were alone, and it was our turn to take care of them. We were very glad and thankful to be together, but the sorrow of all the others surrounded us. On the way, we met Soviet soldiers, starved, dirty, and tired, who were trying to join the defense army in the city of Smolensk. Large groups from our camp decided to go back to Orsha. No one objected, so with one horse and wagon they turned around and left.

We continued pushing east as fast as our tired horses could go. The only three men in our group were Bobovnikov, Father, and Kazik. We traveled on the old rocky country roads that connected villages and cities. These roads had been used by generations of farmers and travelers. The countryside was peaceful and beautiful, full of greenery, wildflowers, trees, and forests. This was, after all, early summer. We were blessed with good sunny weather. Without changes of clothing or protection from rain, bad weather would have been disastrous.

By now I was used to long rides, but I preferred to walk until my feet hurt, enjoying the fresh air and feeling secure at having my parents at my side. With the passing of time and many miles, I detached myself from the past, and the pictures of faces left behind started to fade away. Almost two years had passed since we left Łódź, and war was still going on. We were still wandering, with no home, no possessions, and no destination. I wondered if there would ever be an end to this, and if we would ever have a roof over our heads again. I wondered if one day I would sleep in my own bed, without fear. I also wondered if we'd be alive tomorrow.

In the proximity of Smolensk, we stopped in a kolkhoz where our group was unloaded into a barn. There was plenty of hay, and I was delighted to be able to lie down on fresh-smelling grass after having warm rice and fresh milk, which was a very generous gift from the farmers. By now we looked alike, suntanned, dirty, tired. We were called *bierzency*, which means "refugee" or "one who runs."

I was awakened during the night by the terrifying sound of artillery fire. Father consulted with Bobovnikov, and then we were all on our feet, picking up camp and preparing the horses. As fast as we could, we disappeared into the nearby forest. Artillery could be heard closer and closer, which signified the approaching battle. We were hoping to find space between the two armies to pass through. We walked in the darkness of the forest, calculating our direction by the sound of firearms. I felt a weakness in my legs as we walked in terror. I understood that we were in the midst of the front line of battle and didn't know how we would get out of it.

We advanced silently, staying close to each other. I believe that the horses, sensing the danger, did not make any sound. We walked in the darkness of night for a long time. At last we determined that the artillery fire we heard was a little further away, but still bullets were flying over our heads. We continued pushing ahead until finally we realized that we were leaving the battle behind us and that we had been able to pass through unharmed. Later we heard that Germans had parachuted behind the front lines with heavy artillery and tanks in an effort to surround Smolensk. The Soviet army was able to push the Germans back.

In July, we reached the state borders between Byelorussia and Russia. We proceeded in the direction of Vyaz'ma, hoping to arrive there before the Germans. Luckily for us, milk was easy to obtain from the passing cattle, and with our stores of goods, especially rice, we had feasts. Sometimes if we camped by the river we would wash our clothing one at a time, and I learned that sand could be substituted for soap.

At night we could light a campfire and eat warm food, and we rested our heads on the ground, using our hands as pillows. We did not have tents. I remember falling asleep with the stars above. Since German airplanes seldom attacked at night, we felt relatively safe.

On the way to Vyaz'ma, we passed a town called Glinka, named after a famous composer. We hoped to find a train, but there was none, so we continued on foot.

One evening, we approached a village full of Soviet army soldiers. We were surprised, since we were already quite deep in Russia, not too far from Vyaz'ma and Moscow itself. When he saw women and children refugees, the commanding officer ran to us. "Leave immediately," he said. "Watch out and be prepared for anything that might happen. We are encircled by Germans."

Being so close to safety after so much effort and then to have the Germans catch up with us was our worst fear. With very low spirits and without almost any hope, we did the only thing we could do—we tried to escape. Terribly tired and hungry, we passed ahead on the side roads under the protection of night. We walked seven hours nonstop, and somehow we found holes in every line and passed through unnoticed. Only when we arrived to within nine kilometers of Vyaz'ma did we feel we'd left danger behind.

Vyaz'ma was the last destination of our group. From now on, we were on our own. Bobovnikov's function ended once his refugees were delivered to safety. He distributed the leftover food among us, returned horses and wagons to authorities, and left.

We found lodgings in a mess hall of one of the factories. There we were given some bread and hot wheat cereal. After eating hardtack and water for so long, this was a feast.

Before we even considered our next step, we had to register with the war committee. There was none to be found, however. The committee itself had evacuated to the east. This situation did not sound very good, and we decided that we had to move further inside Russia. Our plan consisted of going to Moscow and then to Gor'kiy. We parted from our group, and the four of us and the Semiaszko family walked to the railroad station in hopes of finding a train. The trains were used only for military personnel, though, to transport armed forces to the front line.

Father did not give up and finally spotted a cargo train with the locomotive pointed in an eastern direction. There was no information about when and where it would go. There was nothing much we could do but wait and see what the morning would bring. That night, we slept on the stone floor of the station waiting room. The next day, to our delight, we found that there was one train going to Tashkent. The warm climate deep in the south part of Russia, far from Germans, looked very attractive to us. Along the open platform was a boxcar, into which we jumped. At least we were under cover and had places on the floor for sleeping.

After a very long wait, I felt the train jerk and then gently start moving forward. The sound of the moving train brought hope that with every roll of the wheels we'd be further and further away from the Germans.

At that moment I heard the roar of approaching airplanes. The train stopped violently. The Germans attacked the station and the terrifying sounds of falling bombs followed by many explosions surrounded us. We were sitting targets. I was overcome by panic. It seemed there was no escape.

Kazik decided to go out of the boxcar and watch the action to keep us informed. "Relax," he said, "an airplane just passed us." Seconds later he said, "Another one is coming; cover your heads." I didn't want to hear this and I begged him to come inside. He laughed at me. "What's the difference where I'm standing," he said, "if the bombs reach us?"

One of the bombs destroyed the railroad track, but with some maneuvering after the attack was over, it was possible to move on. We were still alive and continuing east.

At the station in Penza, unbelievably, there was warm food for refugees. After traveling two more days, we arrived in the larger town of Ruzayevka. The train could not go any further. To be completely safe, however, we preferred to go deeper into Russian territory.

At that point the Semiaszko family decided that they were far enough and prepared to stay in the nearby kolkhoz. Father's mission was fulfilled, as the Semiaszko family was safe.

We boarded another train. This one took us to Arzamas, a little town that looked centuries old. We reported to the official upon our arrival, hoping there would be some place for us. There was not, though, since just a few days earlier a large transport of refugees had arrived there.

Back in the railroad station, we noticed a train on the track. And once again, it was facing east. We jumped into one of the boxcars, not even knowing the destination. Then the train started moving forward. We sat on the floor of the semi-dark boxcar and looked through the wide open door. The train moved very slowly, passing little villages with green fields growing wheat, potatoes, cabbage, and other vegetables, pastures with growing cattle, forests, and meadows filled with rainbows of colorful flowers swaying gently as they were moved by light wind. There were other families traveling just like us, refugees torn by war and misery. Each family had a meager supply of food, mostly dry cereal and dry bread. On unexpected stops, all passengers would run outside, men on one side of the train, women on the other. It was the only place we had to relieve ourselves. During one of these stops, Kazik did not realize that the train had started moving. We saw him running after us, but when the train was turning on a curve, we lost him from our view. I started to cry. Father was trying to calm Mother, and people were trying to assure us that he probably was able to jump into the last boxcar. Everyone was upset, but we had to wait until the next stop to see if he was with us. When we finally stopped, we found Kazik. He did jump on the last boxcar, but he almost lost his pants.

If the train stopped near a stream, we would run to wash our face and hands. There was nothing else to do and we traveled day after day in dirty clothes and with dirty bodies. By now, however, we were past the danger of German air raids, and this knowledge had a soothing effect on all of us.

We didn't have any light to illuminate our boxcar, so at dusk some of us would sit in the open door with our feet hanging out watching the sky get darker and darker as the last rays of sun disappeared on the horizon. Then I would come to our space on the floor and lie down where we'd sleep, one next to the other.

We lived without any possessions, no home, monotonous dry food, no destination—just vagabond refugees resigned to being homeless, dirty, hungry, and exhausted. We were also plagued with lice, which covered our garments and our hair. They were impossible to get rid of.

It was almost the end of July when we arrived at Zelenodol'sk in the Kazan region. This train would go no further. Once again, we were deposited at a small station in the middle of nowhere, with only a little hardtack left and no place to go. After a long search, Father, with his endless energy and optimism, found out that there was a train going to Tomsk, Siberia, and another to Yoshkar Ola in Mari-El Autonomous Republic. It was decided that we would go to Yoshkar Ola, close to the Ural Mountains, because it was far enough east that we felt we would be safe. If the Germans advanced that far, Russia would collapse, in which case it did not matter if we'd be a little further or not.

Again we jumped into a boxcar, with our last sack of food in Father's hand. In this train, we met evacuees from Moscow. We'd had no information, but knowing that Moscow was evacuated meant there was a bad situation on the front. Two weeks later, on the morning of August 7, we arrived in Yoshkar Ola. It was the last stop. I remember only that we were taken to a school building and directed to a Turkish bath. We were each provided with a piece of soap. I remember that it took me a long, long time to remove the dust, dirt, and sweat from my body. It brought unbelievable relief to feel the warm water, even if it was only a small bucketful, which we used to wash our clothes after we washed our bodies. Next we had hot soup and bread. The bread tasted sweet and delicious, even though the color was dark and it felt more like clay. I was sorry to see it gone.

That night, with the rest of the refugees, we slept on the floor of the school auditorium. As always, our hands served as pillows, but at least the constant rocking of the train was gone. It felt strange to sleep in a building after so many weeks on the road.

The next day, Party officials came. Father requested work in the town, but the answer was no. "We have orders," they said, "to employ refugees, but to spread them in different kolkhozes in the provinces."

We were provided with a horse-drawn wagon and again started to walk to the assigned place for our family, some eighty kilometers from Yoshkar Ola, the last train station in the region; trains arrived only once a day, or sometimes only once a week. After hundreds of miles of traveling, eighty kilometers was not so much, but still to walk that distance required two days. We wondered about our destination, walking deeper and deeper into wilderness and deserted regions and forests. We walked all day and in the evening stopped in a small village and slept on the dirt floor of a farmer's hut.

By morning, we started our wandering again, until we reached the town of Toryal, where the executive committee, or Ispolkom, of the local soviet had branches. From there Father was assigned to be a bookkeeper in a kolkhoz named Trudovik in the village of Kuzhnur, still eight kilometers away.

And so we arrived to our final hiding place, the last destination of our wandering journey, hopeful that the Germans would never reach us here. Because if they did, there was no place else to go.

6
LIFE IN THE KOLKHOZ

On August 9 we had been under fire for seven weeks, running from Nazi bullets and air raids. We slept on stone floors, dirt, grass, or mud. We walked through villages, forests, rivers, and country roads, endlessly riding on cattle trains, filthy, hungry, and tired. Finally we saw in the distance a village a little larger than others, descending from a hill nestling in a valley surrounded by forests. Kuzhnur, a kolkhoz in Mari-El Autonomous Republic, was one of the few kolkhozes whose inhabitants were Russian. In all other villages lived very primitive peoples of Mongolian origin, and they had their own language and customs. I discovered that they worshiped wooden gods deep in the forest, which I wanted to find and see for myself, but I was discouraged by other children's gossip that if anyone was caught near these gods, that person would be killed. In such isolated locations, no one would ever know of the dead person's fate. I quickly abandoned this idea.

The kolkhoz consisted of forty-two huts, one family in each hut. All the huts stood in a row on one side of a dirt road. On the other side was a forest descending into a small canyon, at the bottom of which flowed a river. The quietness and tranquility of this place was interrupted only by barking dogs, crowing roosters, or mooing cows. It seemed wonderful to me.

We stopped at a small hut called the office in the kolkhoz courtyard and waited for an official. An old farmer, a manager, appeared. Then we were greeted by more farmers, who came to see refugees from so far away. There was a noticeable absence of young men—only women, children, and elderly men were present. The young ones had been drafted and were serving in the army. The war was felt even here. Fathers, brothers, husbands, and sons were dying

61

in the battles while their women were left in charge of the families and the daily work.

We were assigned to a hut on the edge of the village which belonged to an old farmer, Nikita Ivanovich, and his wife, Ekaterina Ivanovich, who was almost blind. They had refused to join the kolkhoz and because of it had been imprisoned. They were allowed to come back to their home in their later years. Their only son had been sent to vocational school, and their daughter had been sent to work in a factory. These parents mourned their children as though they were dead. I felt terribly sorry for the old couple who, with resignation and resentment, let our family into their hut. We were told to occupy a corner of the room.

The next morning I woke up refreshed and rested. I washed my hands and face with cold water from a little container hanging from the ceiling, which had a bucket under it. It stood in the corner next to the entrance door. Every hut had the same arrangement.

On the rustic table of plain wooden boards lay freshly baked bread. I was ready to run to have some of it when I saw the farmer and his wife kneeling and praying in front of the table. Then I noticed icons, or holy pictures, hanging in the corner above the table. They were also in every hut in this kolkhoz, in spite of pressure and threats of Party officials. Farmers would not give up their belief in God. After finishing praying, Nikita Ivanovich and his wife left the hut to attend to their chores.

We ate, then Father left and I began exploring my new surroundings. Even though it was only the second week of August, the short summer was almost over and fall was approaching. The sun was not as warm, leaves were already turning yellow, and there was a cool morning breeze. I could hear gentle whispers as the leaves moved, and I was sure that I was greeted and welcomed by these quiet old trees. I walked outside to the courtyard. To the left was a barn. A goat was in the pasture and chickens were spread around looking for worms. A cat came to me and started to rub against my feet. Delighted, I picked him up. Behind the barn lay a garden with rows of potatoes, onions, carrots, and other vegetables. Nikita Ivanovich and his wife were bent down working there.

On the other side of the road, bushes of raspberries displayed their rich red colors between green leaves. I started to pick them, swallowing as fast as I could. I was reprimanded, however. The raspberries did not belong to us, I was told, and I could not pick them.

Life on the farm didn't allow time for leisure and rest during the summer. Provisions had to be made to have food for the long winter. From the youngest ones to the oldest, everyone had to work in the fields. I went with other young girls to work on the task of turning over hay, cut previously, to let it dry in the sun. This job was the easiest and cleanest of all, considered by everyone as play accompanied by singing and laughing. At this particular time, the girls had plenty to laugh about—me. They laughed at my lack of knowledge and my handling of the tools we were to use.

All the girls were in assigned rows with rakes to turn grass that was dry on the top so the bottom would be exposed to the sun. This task was done in rhythmical motions, step-turn, step-turn. As this was the first time I'd ever been in the fields, the long rake kept slipping and falling from my hands. After each step, I stopped and tried to turn over a small amount of hay, but instead of staying in a neat little bunch like it was supposed to, my hay spread all over the place. A supervising woman approached and started to teach me but got discouraged. No one had ever seen such clumsiness before. I fell behind in my row, to much teasing and laughter. Humiliated, I continued to work, telling myself to keep going. This I did until the end of the day, when my hands were blistered and my feet hurt. We had to finish so many square feet to earn an hour's work, for which we would be paid like everyone else. I did not make even one hour's work all day long. Children raised on the farm had never been exposed to a city girl and could not understand my ignorance. I walked to our hut alone, not feeling upset or hurt, just tired and hungry. I knew that tomorrow I had to face the same task since it was unacceptable for a healthy girl not to work. I would learn tomorrow. Eventually I did learn the right way of doing it and I was satisfied and proud. I was becoming a farmer's girl. At least I thought I was.

One day I was approached by the girls during the noon break as we were sitting under the shade of a tree. "You are a Jew?" one of them asked me.

"Yes," I answered, surprised.

"Then show us a tail and your horns," she said.

"But I do not have them," was my answer.

"It is not true," she replied. "All Jews have them. Show us how you hide them." All of them started touching my head hoping to find horns and they looked for my tail. I was shocked and was not able to convince them they were mistaken. They believed the traditional Russian anti-Semitism that had been taught for centuries by the Russian Orthodox Church. Not being exposed to a Jewish person before, the image of a Jew they had was of some resemblance to a devil. It was unanimously agreed that I used magic powers to hide the unwanted extremities, in spite of my explanations. Once more I was convinced how difficult it is to be Jewish.

After work, there were still chores to be done. One of them was getting water, which had to be carried from the well located in the center of the village. Water was pulled up by a bucket attached to one end of a rope. The other end was tied to a long round log suspended on two forks with a handle on one side. The bucket was lowered into the well. When it filled up with water it had to be raised by moving the handle to wind the rope around the log. Then, still holding the handle, the bucket had to be pulled out of the well. The water was then transferred into someone's bucket.

Not without difficulty did I learn how to manipulate this primitive well, so simple in method yet so difficult to perform without splashing water on unwanted places. To save time, two buckets of water were carried on each trip. To facilitate carrying them, buckets were attached to the ends of a stick that rested on the shoulders, with hands helping to balance them. The first time, I couldn't accomplish any of this. Not only did I spill water, but I also lost my balance and fell down. I did master it, though, and with time it became easy, at least during the summer. This water was used all day for cooking, drinking, and washing our faces and hands.

Since we had very few garments, washing them was not time consuming. I took our things to the river, and with a little sand sprinkled on the material, I scrubbed them on the rocks and then rinsed them in the clean river. I enjoyed being in the forest sitting with my feet in the cold, fresh water, listening to the birds and daydreaming undisturbed. After washing, I would lay out my own dress to dry in the sun and, once dry, put it back on.

There was also the hut floor to be washed. Once a week with an iron blade, I scrubbed the plain wooden floor, then rinsed it with a wet rag. I used as little water as possible, to save myself trips to the well.

Summer was almost over, and it was time to start preparation for winter. During the summer, the forest is very generous, providing herbs, mushrooms, and berries. Any free time I spent collecting these treasures. It was an easy task and a pleasant one. I became an expert in recognizing poisonous mushrooms, which are the most beautiful. The one I liked most looked like something from a fairy tale. It had a bright red top sprinkled with red dots.

We ate berries at mealtime with some bread and water. Mushrooms, after washing and slicing, were threaded on grass stems and dried under the sun. Later on, in the winter, they provided valuable supplements to our meals.

Life in the kolkhoz was so different from what I'd ever known before. We were completely isolated from the world, forgotten by time and civilization. Orsha seemed to me now like a great capital, and Łódź was dimmed by the passage of time and war. We had stepped from the twentieth century back to the primitive life of hundreds of years before. In these tranquil surroundings, it was almost impossible to comprehend that we were in the same hemisphere, the same country, or the same period of time.

The little information from the Russian front that did reach us was very bad. The Germans were advancing rapidly. Orsha and the road on which we traveled had fallen. But here in the kolkhoz, life continued undisturbed by bombs, with the only worry being about provisions and preparation for a long winter. There was not a store in any of the villages, and even in Toryal nothing was available. We depended totally on our own production of vegetables, wheat, meat, eggs, and milk products, some of which we were permitted to grow ourselves, as long as it did not interfere with the communal work on the farm. We were paid according to workday hours. As newcomers with no food at all, Father had been paid some potatoes and wheat in advance.

As a rule, the kolkhoz had to pay a quota assigned by the government on all the products from the farm. Then farmers were paid, and if by luck there was a surplus of products, the remains of the food was distributed among all the kolkhozniks, the farmers.

It was after this first payment that we faced a big problem. Father brought home a sack of wheat and potatoes. The potatoes were put into the corner of the hut, but the wheat had to be processed into flour and then into bread. Fortunately, some farmers were ready to go to the mill with their own grain, so Father and I picked up a sack of wheat and between the two of us carried it to a horse-drawn wagon and joined the rest of them. The mill was a few miles away, and we walked while the sacks of wheat were pulled by the horse. At the mill, I was completely bewildered. To me, bread was something that you buy. Here was wheat being ground by a stone that was moved by a windmill and it was turned into flour. I wondered how we'd ever be able to bake bread out of this.

With the aid of our farmer host, we got our first lesson. First, we needed starter, which was saved from week to week. Someone gave us our first batch as a welcome present. Then after mixing flour, water, and starter, the mixture was left to rise overnight. The next day it had to be kneaded, which was very hard physically since enough bread was needed to last a whole week. Neither Mother nor I could perform this task, so it became Father's job. After kneading, loafs of round bread were formed and left to rise again. Only then was it ready to be baked.

In the morning, the fire had to be lit in the oven. Since no one had matches, red charcoal was conserved in the oven from one day to the next. If the charcoal died during the night, only the good will of a neighbor would allow one to have fire again.

When the oven was hot, the bread was shoved in to bake. First Ekaterina Ivanovich would bake hers, and then it was our turn. The wonderful smell of freshly baked bread filled the air of the kolkhoz.

To have fire, we needed wood. Nikita and Ekaterina demanded that we help with the logs. The only way to have them was to cut our own tree in the forest, a task we had never performed. Father borrowed a saw and Kazik, Father, and I marched into the forest to cut a tree. With no experience, it was a miracle that we were not killed. By the end of the day, however, a tree was cut and chopped with an ax into logs. Our hands were scratched, bruised, and blistered, and our backs were aching. We still had to transport the logs to our hut. I remember the three of us going back and forth with logs on our backs all the way up the hill to the kolkhoz.

At precisely this time I reached my womanhood. I started with cramps. I sat down and didn't want to move. Father came, ready to go again to pick up more logs. When I didn't follow him and Kazik, but still sat with no intention of proceeding, Father came back and scolded me for sitting and doing nothing. I didn't know how to tell him what was happening to me. This was a very private event not to be discussed. Even Mother did not prepare me for it. I felt hurt and started to cry. Father attributed this to my unwillingness to work and strongly urged me to start picking up logs immediately. Still crying, I stood up and continued carrying logs, doing my best to disregard the cramps and discomfort. To survive in this primitive life was hard, and entering womanhood was just another thing to be done.

As hard as it was in the kolkhoz, it was still far better than being under German occupation. News from the front continued to be bad as the German army continued to advance. Refugees from Moscow had arrived and settled in the vicinity.

At this moment, however, our biggest worry was Kazik, the only young man in the kolkhoz. It was only a matter of time before he would be sent to some factory or drafted. He managed to obtain permission to enter an obscure university near Yoshkar Ola to study forest engineering. Immediately he packed a few loaves of bread and started the seventy-five-kilometer journey on foot. Sad and with heavy hearts, we said goodbye. Life for him would not be easy away from the family. He was provided with living quarters and food, as were the rest of the students. Dorms were very primitive, and for food he was allowed four hundred grams of black heavy bread and watery soup each day—he was starving.

This was too much for Mother to bear. On her own, she filled a sack with some bread, potatoes, and whatever she could find, strapped the sack onto her back, and early one morning left Kuzhnur to walk the seventy-five kilometers to Kazik. Alone, she walked through villages and forests. She stopped at night in kolkhozes she passed through, and after three days of walking she reached Yoshkar Ola, and Kazik. After a few days of rest, she walked back. Only a mother's love could produce the effort required for such an accomplishment.

During the white nights of the northern summer, Kazik walked the seventy-five kilometers to us, nonstop, in one night and half of a day. Then, with some manipulation, Father was able to send Kazik a loaf of bread a week from Toryal. Later on, he was drafted to a Polish army formed in Russia and sent to the first line of fire on the front.

It was time for me to go to school. The only school in our region was six kilometers away, in Toryal. Since school was too far for me to walk to and return back home again every day, we had to find a family that was willing to board me for the school week. One family agreed, but for sixteen kilograms of grain a month. For this, I had a corner on the floor in the only room of the little house where the father, mother, and a son lived.

In September, I took a loaf of bread and some potatoes and started my first of many walks to school. The first night in my new home was very lonely. The hut was very simple. All my possessions were on a small shelf, the bread and potatoes and a small iron pot. I sat on the floor in my corner of the room facing the family as they sat around the table during their evening meal. Apparently I was not to eat with them. I didn't want to be there, ignored by strange people who were indifferent if I was hungry or if I prepared myself something to eat or not. As the sun was setting and the gray of early evening covered the earth, my spirits also fell into darkness. Finally, my stomach demanded some food. I got up, peeled a potato, put it in my pot, covered it with water, and stuck it in the oven still hot after being used by the family. I ate my potato with a slice of bread and drank a little milk diluted with water. I washed my wooden spoon and bowl, put them away, crawled into my straw bed and cried myself to sleep.

7
A BITTER WINTER

Toryal was a small town, but it did have a post office, a government official building, a school, and a hospital. The post office was a hut with a sign on it. The government building was a small brick house. The hospital was a wooden structure with two rooms filled with rows of beds for the patients, a doctor's office with no visible medicine, and a dentist's office available only for the extraction of sore teeth.

The school building was a log cabin similar to the huts, but it had enough rooms for each class, with rows of desks that seated two students each, a blackboard, and a table and chair for the teacher.

When I entered the school, I felt confident of myself. I was one of the few refugees who joined the regular kolkhoz students, and we were all strangers. There were children from Kiev, Moscow, and Leningrad (now St. Petersburg), all of which were coming under German attack. We all dressed in shabby clothing, and we all had stomachs that were not full.

From the very beginning, I was ahead of the class and assumed a leadership role, much to the delight of the young and inexperienced teachers—all of whom were women. The most capable female teachers and all the male teachers were used for military needs, so our education left a lot to be desired. We lacked books, and those few that we had, we shared. We used old scraps of printed paper to write on, and wrote between the printed lines. To our credit, most of us tried to cooperate and help in any way we could, especially by helping the students who came from Mari families, because they spoke poor Russian. For many of these children, this was their first time away from home. It was not easy for any of us.

Our education was divided into two parts. First, we continued with Communist indoctrination. Second, we were trained for military fitness. Every day we were drilled as young cadets would be, beginning with the youngest ones. My age group began more advanced training. We were taught to disassemble, clean, reassemble, and use firearms. Later on, we were trained in tanks and armed vehicles. Tremendous human losses on the battlefields forced everyone to be ready when needed for defense, and we had to be prepared. Old and young, we were ready to help liberate humanity from Nazi brutality. I was ready and eager to do it. I even tried to enlist in the army and went as far as the recruiting office in Toryal. Needless to say, I was advised to go back to my studies and first finish school. And then, if still needed, I'd be advised of the next steps to take. I needed more years to grow up.

I continued with the everyday routine of school work, learning, helping others, preparing meager meals of potatoes and bread for myself. I did have a problem with my clothes, especially shoes, because I was outgrowing everything. My dress didn't matter as much as the shoes, which were too small. I finally learned to walk barefooted, as many others did.

Then came an unexpected package from our aunt in Gor'kiy. This arrival was a real treasure! She sent two pillows, some very old clothes, a winter coat for both my parents, and a pair of shoes for me. Excitedly I picked up the beautiful old brown shoes and tried to put them on. To my enormous disappointment, they were too small. I continued trying to squeeze my foot in, desperately hoping that somehow I'd be able to wear them. While I did manage to put them on, I was unable to walk. So the illusion of having a new pair of old shoes evaporated.

Approaching winter could be seen and felt as days became shorter. The wind changed direction and started blowing from the north, bringing with it cooler air. The sun frequently disappeared behind the clouds, bringing gray and rainy days. The last of the crops was stored away. Logs were piled against the hut walls, ready to be used later. Foods such as potatoes and onions were accommodated in the cellar. Soon it was too cold to be barefooted, and once again the trees in the forest provided help.

After trees were cut down, the bark was carefully peeled off and cut into long strips. These strips were soaked and stretched and dried. Then they were braided, four strips at a time, and formed into

Sandals of the type Hanna wore in Kuzhnur.

a kind of sandal. The strips were held together by sewing with a thin thread made of the same strips. This thread was also used to make rope, which would tie around shoes and legs in order to keep them on the feet. To protect feet from being scratched by these very rough shoes, scraps of material were wrapped around feet.

By trading an amount of grain to a farmer who made these shoes, we obtained protection for our feet. The only problem we were facing now was the lack of material with which to wrap our feet and legs. Somehow we found old rags, and then we were ready for fall. I paraded around our room in my new footwear, hardly able to walk in these stiff wooden sandals that would not bend. After some amount of practice, I learned.

At the beginning of the school week, I would pick up a loaf of bread and a few potatoes and onions. Since I had to walk through the dense forest where wild animals lived, especially wolves, I also carried with me bells that made noise, which was supposed to scare the wolves and keep them away from me. It was known that hungry wolves would attack humans, especially children.

Then I would start for school. At the end of the kolkhoz road I turned right. For some time, the road passed through empty camps. Then it reached the forest, turned left, and gradually disappeared through the trees. At the beginning of this road daylight filtered through the leaves of trees, forming different shadows that danced in the breeze. Then the trees became more dense and daylight almost disappeared. I was uneasy and scared of the gray darkness surrounding me, especially on overcast or rainy days. Alone, I followed the path, not daring to step off of it for fear of becoming lost or disoriented.

I learned to distinguish different sounds of animals, especially the sweet happy songs of birds or their calls of distress, at which case I was on the alert. My favorite one was the cuckoo bird, with his chirp of "coo-coo" repeated many times. Superstition was that counting a large amount of coo-coos would bring good luck, so I counted every time I heard them.

A small kolkhoz of about fifteen or twenty huts marked the halfway point for me. I always felt better when I reached it, knowing that I had only three kilometers more to walk. At the other edge of the forest, daylight appeared again. After turning to the left, there was a straight road to Toryal. At the end of the week I traveled the same road but in the opposite direction, emerging from the forest and walking down the hill to our kolkhoz, where my parents would be waiting for me with warm food and an even warmer welcome.

Early in September, the first flakes of snow started falling, a sign that winter was around the corner. I walked home that day on a slippery road, wondering how difficult winter would be. My feet were wet and cold because of melting snow, which penetrated the wooden sandals.

As I was leaving the village that marked the halfway point in the forest, I started feeling uncomfortable, sleepy, and aching. I was afraid to sit and rest because I might fall asleep, which would be a very dangerous thing to do. I had to reach home before darkness. I rang my bells constantly to keep myself awake and to keep the wolves away. All I wanted was to open the door to the warmth of our home and to be with my parents. The thought of this pushed me ahead. I dragged my feet to the end of the forest and finally down the hill, reaching our house completely exhausted. One look told my parents that I was sick.

During that night I burned with fever. In the morning I had cramps and nausea and was throwing up. The next day my condition worsened, and I had to run outside constantly. With no outside house, I was fully exposed to cold, wet weather. To give me some protection, Mother would cover me with her coat, which helped a little. The following day I was even worse. We did not have a thermometer, but my fever was very high and I was not improving. I became weak and couldn't hold down anything, even water. Since lice were our constant companions, it was feared that I had typhus.

My parents became desperate. Father went to Toryal, hoping to find a doctor. In the hospital, one young doctor had pity on him and agreed to come and see me. She was a young woman just out of medical school, only one of two attending physicians in the hospital. Doctors were needed in the military for wounded soldiers on the battle front, so few were left for the rest of the country. This doctor came as a friend, for moral support. She examined me, but even she was not sure of a diagnosis. She was without any kind of medication and had no experience. She offered to take me to the hospital so I could be in bed instead of on the floor, but she warned that I could be exposed to secondary infections there, since I would have to share a bed with another girl. There was an epidemic of scarlet fever and typhus.

Other than a bed, the hospital was of no advantage because there was no medication and there was a tremendous shortage of nurses. As my parents were debating what to do, I cried and begged not to go. I preferred to run outside and sleep on the floor as long as I could stay home. Everyone agreed to leave me where I was and let nature take its course. The doctor left after prescribing rice and sugar. Father went in search of it and came back empty handed. The only available food was the same dark bread and potatoes. Mother started brewing tea for me by soaking dry bread, but my stomach would not tolerate it. I was getting weaker and was becoming dehydrated.

I couldn't get up without help. Peasant women would stop by and advise my mother, "Let her go. God needs an angel." Mother wouldn't give up, though. I remember her sitting by my side and playing solitaire with a deck of cards that she found somewhere. When she was winning, she would say to me, "You see, everything is going to be fine." When she was losing, she would cheat a little and win again. There was no losing for her.

I felt very sick and had reached the point that I no longer cared what happened. I didn't want to have cramps or nausea, and I didn't want to be carried under the tree during frequent attacks. I knew that I was very close to death.

I guess God didn't need this angel, because during the night I broke into a sweat, the fever broke, and by morning I started feeling better. I heard farmers whispering that a miracle had happened. Whatever the reason, and I don't ask why, I got well.

When I was fully recovered, I went back to school and resumed the routine of life on the farm. In the sanctuary of tranquility, peacefulness, and beauty in this remote part of the world removed from civilization, life continued basically unchanged. Yet there was a brutal war going on and its tentacles reached us, too. The burden of heavy farm work lay on the shoulders of women, young and old. Most of the men were on the front lines, and most of the young single women were needed in the production of war materials in the factories.

With every infrequent letter from Kazik, we rejoiced for a short time. Letters traveled very slowly, and at the time we would receive one, we wondered of his current well-being. We knew he was on the first line of battle and thus we constantly worried about him. Added to that, we didn't know the destiny of Marie and her family and all our friends. We grieved, fearing the worst.

We were able to contact Grandmother Raquel and the rest of our Russian family. They were evacuated from Moscow to Tashkent, deep inside Russia, and we learned that they were safe. Father requested and obtained permission for his brother David to come as a bookkeeper in one of the neighboring kolkhozes. At this point, we didn't worry about the NKVD and their investigations of Father's past.

There were terrible losses of humans in battles, and the advancing German troops were the main and only preoccupation of the government and citizens. Germans advancing to Stalingrad (now Volgograd) could bring disaster to the whole civilized world. If Stalingrad fell, there would be nothing to stop Hitler from conquering all of

U.S.S.R. and then the rest of Europe. In the midst of this dark scenario, we entered into the cruel winter of 1942.

At that time, one of the very oldest huts became vacant. Usually, generation after generation lived in the same hut. Since this hut was empty, we jumped at the opportunity to have it for our own, much to the delight of the owner of the hut in which we were living. I remember scrubbing the dirty floor and clearing the walls of spiders and cockroaches. We patched holes in the walls with fresh moss and moved in. An old table and bench were left in the hut, so all we needed was straw with which to make our beds. We brought our only wooden bowl from which we shared our food, three wooden spoons (one for each of us), three clay mugs, a pot in which to cook potatoes, and, most valuable of all, red charcoal to start our own fire in the oven. These amounted to all our possessions.

Now we were in our own home for the first time since the war started. It felt great, but there were big problems, too. We needed dry wood for fire; we only had new logs, freshly cut. Logs need two years to dry. When we started our first fire, the hut filled with smoke from wet logs that wouldn't flame. Finally Father borrowed some dry logs from the office and we accomplished the task of warming our cabin. For the rest of our stay in the kolkhoz, having a continuous fire became our biggest concern and required our greatest efforts. Fire was one of the main means of surviving the winter.

We stored a few potatoes in the cellar and sacks of grain in the corner. Then we realized we had uninvited guests who liked to share our grain—mice, lots of them. Fortunately, I received as a gift a black kitten which I became very fond of and terribly attached to. The kitten returned my affection by proudly bringing me the mice he caught.

The first heavy snowstorm transformed the world into a fairy-tale wonderland of peacefulness, beauty, and serenity. The forest and ground were covered thickly by a sparkling blanket under which even the huts disappeared.

We were told of the severity of the winter in this part of Russia, but we were not prepared for what came. Once the snow was on the ground, it stayed there for nine long months. The accumulation of it became a nightmare. Roads disappeared under it. Only narrow paths led from one hut to another. Sometimes in the morning, windows and doors were blocked by snow that had to be cleared by shoveling it one step at a time. Hungry wolves in packs would venture into the village during the night looking for prey, howling their long songs under our windows. Many times I would look through the window and face them eye to eye. I admired their beauty and power and was thankful to be inside. I didn't dare go out, even if I needed to.

Days became shorter and shorter until each lasted only a few hours, from about nine in the morning until about two in the afternoon. To light our hut, we used long resinous strips stuck between the logs of the walls. Since we just had a limited amount of these, we only burned one at a time, usually during the evening meal. After eating we sat in darkness for some time before going to sleep. During this time of endless darkness, I learned to dream and transport myself to the imaginary world of growing up. I would meet friends during elaborate parties and dances, using descriptions from Mother's youthful stories for my daydreams. From the need of contact with the opposite sex, I created a boyfriend with whom I carried on one-way conversations, declarations of love, a first kiss, and waltzing in elegant ballrooms full of light and delicious food. Illusions of such rich detail and intensity repeated themselves every night to the point that they became real to me. I would impatiently await night so I could feel the dancing and kisses, taste the food, and smell the perfume of a young girl in love. Each morning, however, I would awake to a cold, hungry, and lonely world.

As the days became shorter and nights longer, temperatures fell lower. The wind became cold to the point that no amount of cloth could protect our bodies, especially not our poor and meager wardrobe. Special shoes called *valenki,* made of very thick felt in the form of a boot, became our first necessity, since the wooden sandals would freeze in a few seconds once exposed to the intense cold. To obtain *valenki* we were forced to turn to the black market. Trading on the black market was one of the worst crimes in the U.S.S.R., punishable by forced labor in Siberia. Yet it couldn't be stopped. Transactions were held in secluded places where goods changed owners. In exchange for sixteen kilograms of grain, it was possible to obtain *valenki,* not necessarily new, but still usable. Obviously the owner of a pair of them was desperately in need of bread. Since Father was doing bookkeeping in neighboring kolkhozes, for which he was paid in grain, we had an excess of grain. We were able to exchange the grain for shoes, after carefully looking around to be sure that no one saw our procedure. With our feet protected from frostbite in our *valenki,* we were able to walk outside. The *valenki* came just in time, since the temperature was falling rapidly and the winter was fierce beyond normal. The only way for me to go to school was on skis, which were loaned by the kolkhoz. So at the beginning of the school week I put on all available clothing, covering my head and exposing only my eyes. Then my coat went on with a wool scarf tied around my neck and under my arms. My bundle of bread and potatoes hung over my shoulder. Next, my skis were tied to the *valenki* with rope. I said good-bye to my parents, and off I went. I crossed all six kilometers sounding my bells constantly. I think I must have looked like a shuffling mummy and would have probably frightened a whole pack of wolves.

In school, there was not much to relieve the cold. Without wood to warm the classroom, we attended classes with coats and gloves on. We would interrupt lessons every so often to run around in order to warm up, and then we'd continue again. We did as much as we could to continue our education. As poor as it was, it was better than no education at all.

After school, back in my rented corner of the hut, I would warm up and eat potatoes that I cooked before I left for school, then return to my dreams as the host family went to sleep also. Winter was very cruel as severe snowstorms paralyzed traffic. Horse-drawn sleds and skis became the only viable transportation. The temperature dropped to more than fifty degrees Celsius below zero.

At this point it was impossible to sit in the classroom and we were dismissed from school. To me, this was a perfect opportunity to go home. Without thinking, I bundled myself with all my rags and happily got on the way. At first running felt comfortable, but very soon freezing air started penetrating my clothing. In order to breathe, I had to cover my nose completely, since moisture froze immediately with each intake of air. After one kilometer my eyes started hurting. I covered them, leaving only small openings in order to be able to see. Then my legs started freezing, so I rubbed them with snow to relieve them. But in doing so my hands became numb. After two kilometers I started feeling frostbite; I knew it manifested itself with loss of feeling. I ran the next kilometer as fast as I could to reach the village in the forest. By the time I reached the first hut and the peasant woman opened the door for me, I was about ready to collapse. She took me in, started rubbing all my body with snow, and scolded me for my foolishness. I drank hot water and finally my circulation was restored. But I still had three kilometers to go.

I refused the offer to stay with the family and stubbornly continued my walk. The next three kilometers were a nightmare. Feeling pain in my legs and arms, I rubbed them with snow. Finally I lost sensibility and I knew I had frostbite in the lower part of my back. I managed to reach Kuzhnur and, when I opened the door to our hut, Mother just stood up and looked at me, not believing her eyes. There was no time for scolding. She grabbed me, undressed me, and rubbed all parts of my body that were turning white from lack of circulation, to avoid gangrene. I was sick for quite some time, but the worst of it was that I could not sit for even a longer time.

In the kolkhoz lived an old woman, Anfisa Zakharevna, who in her youth was a nurse in the czar's army. Her brother was the kolkhoz manager. She took Mother under her protection and was the only person who could really communicate with her. Anfisa was a big help because, during this brutal winter with its endless nights—and without her art—Mother fell into a deep depression. The prolonged darkness and enclosure in the huts commonly produced depressions, even hallucinations. Mother became a victim of such depression and her health started to deteriorate. Anfisa constantly advised me to take care of Mother if I wanted her to live. I became desperately worried, not knowing what I could do to save her. This feeling haunted me for many years. My mother never was able to completely recover from this terrible experience.

Father, on the contrary, adapted himself to this new life in the kolkhoz, happy to be in a remote area safe from the NKVD in this isolated part of Russia. He made friends with farmers who respected him and sought his advice. He was an efficient worker and an excellent bookkeeper. He was asked to supervise a few other kolkhozes in the area and present the results in Toryal. On these occasions, we'd walk together from Kuzhnur to Toryal, counting the telegraph poles that stood on the side of the road—sixteen in each kilometer, ninety-six in all. Sometimes we sang at the top of our lungs in the otherwise still and silent kingdom of the snow-covered forest.

During the winter, activities on the farm came almost to a standstill, except for chores around the house, bookkeeping and office work for Father, and school for me. I felt quite comfortable in my class because I'd become a teacher's helper and had earned respect from my classmates. They were not my friends, but they were not my enemies either. I was always ready to help them, which was appreciated. Almost all the students were honest and completely used to a simple life filled with hard work. A few students were children of Party leaders and government officials appointed to the Toryal region. These children were Russian and had enjoyed a better life, better education, and better clothing. They had access to better food. They formed the elite of society, despite the fact that under Communism all citizens were supposed to be equal.

In my class was a boy, a son of a Party chairman, the highest official position in the Communist party. This boy was known as an aggressive troublemaker. Once he kicked a girl in the abdomen with such ferocity that he perforated her intestine. Unfortunately nothing could be done for her in Toryal since the hospital was not equipped for surgery. A few days later the girl died. She also was a child of a Party official, but a lesser one. After the commotion, anger, and accusations, the parents of the dead girl were transferred to another town, leaving the Party chairman and his son untouched. The boy continued in our school until the end of the school year. We were all terribly upset about this injustice and attended the girl's funeral, which was the only thing we could do for her. No one could protest against the Communist Party. A mother's lamentations didn't count and were ignored by Party leaders. The girl's mother had only one small, pitiful consolation. She declared during her daughter's funeral, "My girl died so clean. No lice were found on her body."

During the endless winter months, it was impossible to keep up with sanitary conditions. On rare occasions we were able to take a bath in the bath hut of our friend, Filip Zakharevich. This hut was very small, with an anteroom and a second tiny room that held two primitive benches (one on top of another), and two barrels (one with cold water, the other with hot). On the dirt floor lay a pile of stones heated with wood. Hot stones were thrown into the water to keep the water hot. After the heated stones became red hot, water was splashed on them to create very hot steam and vapor. The water had to be carried to the hut by buckets, lots of them. Carrying buckets during the freezing weather on slippery ground was not easy. Many times I would slide and stumble, particularly as the path to the bath hut was downhill and my hands felt frozen. If I spilled water, I had to go back to the well, pull more water out, and start walking all over again. Wood had to be brought, too. Father and I cut wood in pieces, then chopped it with an axe until it was ready for the fire. Once the fire was going and the stones and water were hot, then the bath was ready.

We would undress in the open anteroom, which was freezing cold in the winter. Then we would step into the steamed room and take a bath, rubbing our bodies with hot water. We had no soap. We poured almost steaming water over our heads, bringing temporary relief from itching caused by lice bites. Unfortunately the lice couldn't be eliminated, neither by freezing cold nor steaming hot water. They loved to live inside the seams of our clothing, and in our hair.

After our bath we had to enter the open anteroom again, exposing ourselves to bitter cold air, which was shocking to our naked hot bodies. I used to dress quickly and run to our hut. Father would tolerate this form of bathing reasonably well, but for Mother, it was almost too much to bear. However, she had no other choice, so she continued to bathe in this manner, even when it made her sick and weak.

8

THE MOVE TO YOSHKAR OLA

In spite of our being so isolated in this remote part of Russia, news from the fronts occasionally reached us. In the winter of 1942 we heard that although the German army had still not succeeded in its Moscow offensive, it had, by turning south, conquered Kiev (now Kyyiv) and Khar'kov (now Kharkiv) and was proceeding toward Stalingrad. This approach greatly increased our concern for the future. Letting the Germans inside Russia, we were told, was carefully planned by our beloved Stalin, so they would be encircled and destroyed. As beautiful as it sounded, we couldn't believe it, especially since we heard that human losses were enormous, cities were destroyed, and refugees from the war zone were living in misery. Kazik was still on the front line, but we didn't know where. Occasionally letters from him would arrive, but they were dated from five or six weeks before. Later on his letters stopped coming and we lost contact with him completely.

Slowly winter was losing its grip, and once again sun rays started warming our frozen world, melting snow and ice. Beautiful icicles that hung from the roofs started dripping, their majestic grace melting slowly. Trees started shedding blankets of snow, exposing bare branches. Snow on the ground melted and changed from its clean whiteness to a mixture of snow and dirt. We welcomed the smell of spring with its warm air. The kolkhoz was awakening once again to a short and busy summer. Finally the roads were free of snow. They became muddy and slippery after the first spring shower, and walking to school was unpleasant and difficult. Mud and puddles were everywhere.

Every family, including ours, was entitled to a small plot behind their hut. We thus became real farmers burdened with the heavy physical work of preparing the soil inch by inch with a shovel so it was ready for us to plant rows of potatoes, carrots, onions, garlic, and cabbage. Surprisingly, Mother was able to endure this backbreaking work almost single-handedly. I was at school and Father worked for Ispolkom, a governmental branch that had requested him for work in Toryal. Now he divided his time between the kolkhoz and Toryal. For his work there, he received the salary of four hundred grams of bread a day. He also had to instruct new bookkeepers who replaced mobilized men: These were young women, some of whom didn't speak Russian. For this, he was paid sixteen kilograms of rye. He carried sacks of grain on his back all the way home.

Our vegetable garden had to be tended constantly. We had to eliminate weeds, clear new leaves from a starving army of worms, and water our plants. Our hands were unaccustomed to this work and became rough and achy. Seeing the fruits of our work brought hope for a better supply of food, however.

We bought a goat with sixteen kilograms of grain, dreaming of having a steady supply of milk. Our goat grazed with the kolkhoz herd, but slept in our hut. Every morning the goat had to be milked and every morning we hoped for glasses of fresh milk. To our disappointment, though, our goat would not produce more than a half a cup a day. We used this milk with potatoes, and I suspected that Mother stirred a little more milk into my portion.

One day, Father came home with a squealing sack on his back. To Mother's horror, and to my delight, he had a tiny piglet. For the piglet and me, it was love at first sight. With time, Pig and I became inseparable. Everywhere I went, Pig would follow. I fed him cooked grain, potato peels, and, in the beginning, tiny amounts of goat milk. In no time at all, Pig grew large. I had a small problem with him, though. When it was time for me to go to school, he would follow me and I had to take him home. He would escape somehow, and before I would realize it, I heard his squealing behind me. When Mother tried to hold him, he would fight until she had to let him loose. Then he charged after me. I'd scold him and take him home again, then run back to school. When I came home from school, I was welcomed by one extremely happy pig, a cat, and later on, a beautiful rooster. I dearly loved my animals. How patiently they listened to my complaints! They were devoted and loving friends.

The smell of wet soil after spring showers permeated the air. Flowers started to bloom, and the forest was covered with fresh greenery. Birds returning for the summer filled the air with a symphony of singing. School was almost over and we were dismissed early so young people could help in the fields because there was a shortage of working hands.

At that time, I decided to cut my braids. Although I was ready for short hair, I didn't think my parents were, so I did this on my own. There was a woman in Toryal who cut hair, so one day I braided my hair for the last time and with determination walked to her shop. In a few minutes, it was done. My long braids lay on the counter, and I looked into the mirror and saw a strange face with different hair. I picked up my braids, tied the ends together, put them in the sack which held my belongings, and headed home. It's hard to describe the look on my parents' faces when I walked into the hut. I handed my braids to Mother and twirled on my toes, laughing.

During the summer we worked from sunrise to sunset, tending fields in the kolkhoz and our own vegetable garden, preparing for another winter. Our backs ached from being bent all day. The rye and wheat had to be cut mostly by hand, since there were few working tractors available. Grass was cut by sickle, dried, and then stored for feeding animals. Wood was cut for fire. There was no time for rest during the short summer.

Before we realized it, summer was fading away. Once again, the northern winds started blowing and rainy, muggy, gray days were frequent. Autumn was upon us and it was time to start school again, walking through the dark forest. I put on my old pair of *valenki* and worn-out winter clothing, still covered with lice, and started the routine of winter life again. I missed the warm sun and the long summer days, the beautiful flowers, and the singing of birds. There were no more sweet and juicy berries to eat in the forest. Neither were there any more fresh mushrooms.

Every year that passed by left Mother in a worse state of mind. She was overworked and depressed without her art. Worst of all, she was without any news from Kazik and the family we left in Poland. Winter started with terrible severity, and farmers predicted the worst winter ever.

In Toryal, 1943, Hanna (right) in borrowed clothing and
valenki, thick felt boots to protect from frostbite. The boy was
drafted in ninth grade, shortly after this picture was taken. He
died in battle.

We continued with our school work and with our military preparations. I learned how to use a rifle, take it apart, clean it, and put it
back together. I learned to shoot, and we practiced shooting targets.
I learned about tanks, how to distinguish airplanes, and how to dig
trenches. We had cross-country ski drills. We were being prepared to
fight if necessary. Some of my schoolmates who became old enough
were drafted. We bade them goodbye, knowing that many would
never come back. Then the German army encircled Stalingrad and
we faced some of the blackest days ever.

We lost part of our vegetables due to improper storage, so once again potatoes, bread, and water became our daily food. There was a shortage of grain in the kolkhoz, and to stretch it out, dried grass was mixed with rye and then bread was made from this mixture. This bread was a greenish mud color, very heavy and bitter tasting and without salt. While some regions had plenty of salt, this staple in the Mari-El Autonomous Republic was impossible to obtain because of lack of transportation and distribution. I started to show symptoms of vitamin deficiency. I stopped growing, my monthly flow stopped, and my teeth started to decay. I had one tooth infection after another, swollen cheeks, and pain that couldn't be eased because there was no medication of any kind. I had to endure, crying with pain until nature took its course and the abscess under the tooth ruptured, bringing relief from the pain. Then the tooth cracked and fell out, however, leaving the roots still inside the gum. I lost many molars that winter.

My fingers got infected, forming abscesses on top of the joints. I found scraps of material and made bandages so I was able to cover the sores. At night, I would wash them without soap. After they dried, I would cover my fingers again. I remember how painful it was and how difficult it became to do chores that had to be done, even simply peeling potatoes. There was nothing that could be done to help. Only during the long nights could I retreat to my imaginary world and dream of a life of well-being with a warm house and plenty of food, friends, comfortable shoes, and clothing.

The prediction of the farmers turned out to be right. Winter entered with terrible snowstorms during which visibility was almost zero, making it impossible to walk. Mornings after a storm, the huts were completely covered with snow. It was a frightening experience to wake up and see our little window covered with snow. I was scared of being buried under the snow and not being able to open the door to the outside. With Father and myself pushing the door, we would dig in the snow forming a small path that would lead to the road outside the hut. The siege of Stalingrad increased our anxiety for survival, since there was no other place to escape to.

When it looked like the darkest hour for us, the first good news came from the battle front: The Russian army had successfully encircled the German troops, then formed a second ring around them, completely blocking the Nazis, who were attempting to take the city of Stalingrad. After a battle of incredible ferocity and terrible losses of life, for the first time since the war started the Germans were forced to surrender, which was very much against Hitler's orders. The fighting in Stalingrad continued from house to house, greatly increasing the number of dead and wounded soldiers and civilians. The ferocity of the winter contributed to the Russians' advances, since the Germans were not accustomed to these bitter freezes and snowstorms. In the end, after many years of war and defeat, Stalingrad was liberated. Victory was overwhelming.

The heroism and love for Russia displayed by soldiers and civilians alike cannot be denied or ignored. They were defending their country, not Communism. We celebrated the victory at Stalingrad, which was the beginning of the end for Germany. We could stop worrying about Nazi advances deeper in Russian territory, and we no longer feared falling into their hands.

School continued, but my *valenki* began to wear out. As long as I was traveling through the forest on skis, they held out. I got used to being cold and learned to stop and rub my face or hands or any part of my body that felt too numb in order to restore circulation so I could avoid frostbite. I learned to follow snow-covered paths in the forest by heart, to stop being afraid of walking home or to school, and not to be concerned about wolves.

One day, upon approaching our hut as I returned from school, I heard a commotion inside. I ran, and to my delight I saw mama goat in the middle of the room and two beautiful kids jumping up and down on the benches and table. I was as happy as I could be playing with these two little babies, interrupted only by a jealous cat. The kids had to stay inside the hut because of the bitter cold. In fact, that night we had to bring Pig inside, too, so he would not freeze to death.

I didn't mind sharing our hut with my friends, but I think it was too much for my mother. She said she absolutely refused to live, sleep, and eat with the animals under our small roof. Even she was hopeful, though, that our goat would produce milk for all of us. Instead, there was hardly enough for the two kids. And we still had to feed mama goat, Pig, the cat, and our rooster. I guess that in spite of a few years on the kolkhoz, we never really became farmers. We didn't know the correct way to plant, harvest, or store our supply of goods, and we sure didn't know how to make a goat produce more milk.

Father's expert work as a bookkeeper didn't go unnoticed by the Ispolkom. Competent workers were badly needed in offices at Yoshkar Ola, and he was approached by a Party secretary with orders to take a position there. With grave concern, he had to accept this job. His concern was that now we had to leave the sanctuary of the kolkhoz, far removed from the NKVD and Party headquarters, and would again be exposed to the possibility of new investigations into his past. This job "offer" was not a matter of choice. Orders had to be obeyed. Father was given time to transfer his books to a new bookkeeper, and at the end of the school year we planned to move to Yoshkar Ola.

At this time students in my class were being indoctrinated and encouraged to join a Communist youth organization called Komsomol, and it was expected that all of us would apply for membership. During the weekend, my parents and I discussed all the possibilities, talking late into the night, trying to decide what steps I should take. No choice was good. Not accepting the high honor of being in the Komsomol would bring suspicions, and accepting could bring an investigation of my family's past that could end in arrest and imprisonment in Siberia for the rest of our lives. This was a sleepless night. Could it be that after all we'd gone through to survive, we would end in disaster anyway? Finally it was decided that I would join the Komsomol and take the chance that with the confusion and priority of the war demands, my application would be accepted with dozens of others.

I filled in the application, which looked very impressive, but I was glad I didn't have to swear with my hand on a Bible that I stated the truth and only the truth. I handed the application to the Party official with steady hands, but my heart was beating out of control. After a few weeks, a ceremony was held and I was congratulated as a new Komsomol member and presented with a membership card. I never accepted this affiliation that was forced upon me, but I kept my feelings to myself and shared them only with my parents.

Another winter came and went, and then the spring. During the breaks at school, I worked in the kolkhoz. If a tractor was available, I helped with it to prepare fields for planting; I separated grain from the cut wheat stems by beating the stems with sticks attached to each other with string; I tended animals. At the end of school, I bade farewell to the family in whose hut I'd lived and to my schoolmates and teachers. I put my pot and spoon and a few other belongings in a sack. Carrying my sack on my back, I took the path from Toryal to Kuzhnur for the last time.

To obtain permission to move the family, Father had to travel to Yoshkar Ola by himself. He took advantage of a kolkhoz shipment of produce that had to be given as a tax to the government and went to Yoshkar Ola with the horse-pulled cart and one of the kolkhoz members. The trip took about two days walking one way, about seventy-five kilometers in all. Once he had fulfilled the obligation demanded of him by the kolkhoz, he went to the Ministry of Agriculture. There he was met by the secretary of the personnel department, who promised to find living quarters for the family eventually. Meanwhile, Father had to live in his office and sleep on his desk. He obtained coupons for bread and other products, all of which were rationed. After registering his passport with the military, he was ready to start his new job. Two weeks later, Father's patience and his back were both worn out, but his complaints led to nothing, and too much complaining would not be good. About two more weeks passed, then a high-ranking party official obtained a nice apartment in a new building and his old apartment was given to us. Father was given ten days leave to move his family from Kuzhnur. He walked back to us from Yoshkar Ola, averaging thirty-seven kilometers a day.

There was not too much packing to do. Father's friend Filip arranged a wagon and horse for us. We loaded Pig, three sacks of flour, the mama goat with her two kids, and the rest of our belongings onto the wagon. The whole kolkhoz was in front of our hut to see us off. They walked with us to the end of the kolkhoz, bidding us tearful goodbyes. We were on our way to Yoshkar Ola, closing this long episode of being peasant farmers.

Each of us left in a different state of mind. Mother was relieved to end this terribly primitive life and hard work. Father welcomed the change to live in a bigger town, but was sad to leave friends that he he'd made with these simple and honest farmers. I was concerned about changing schools and also knew I would miss the forest, with its tranquil beauty and open spaces. I had gotten used to a farmer's life, but above all else I didn't want to wander ever again. I was happy to stay in one place, wherever it was.

As we were leaving, my kitten got loose from my arms and ran away. I couldn't find him and was forced to leave him behind. We had lost our rooster a few weeks before our departure, when he was attacked and wounded by a hawk. Mother heard the commotion in front of the hut, ran out, and, realizing what was happening, chased the hawk. The rooster didn't survive, however. In spite of my tears over losing our rooster, our stomachs were very happy after a banquet of chicken soup. Poor rooster, he provided us with many, many meals.

Our walk to Yoshkar Ola was very slow. We had to stop and rest frequently because of Mother. It took us three days until we finally arrived at our new quarters. Along the way, we slept in farmers' huts.

When we arrived in Yoshkar Ola, we went to our quarters. We entered a long courtyard, at the end of which stood a wooden house built like a hut, but it was actually much larger. On the right stood a wooden outhouse and a little farther down there was a barn. We unloaded our animals and secured them in a corner of the barn that had been assigned to us. Then we entered the hall of the house. This hall was actually a small, square room with a stove in the middle and four doors leading to four apartments. Each apartment consisted of one-and-a-half very small rooms. We opened our door and entered our apartment.

The white paint over thin wooden walls was peeling, and the rough wooden floors were very dark and dirty. There was a small window on one of the walls, which faced grass and some trees. We felt we had entered civilization again, though, because there was a single light bulb hanging on a cord from the ceiling. Water, however, still had to be carried from the well.

We made our straw bed on the floor, hung our coats on a peg in the wall, and stacked four sacks of flour in the back room. A small shelf accommodated our pot, our bowl, and our three wooden spoons. Later on we obtained a simple table and a bench. We were ready to continue on our path of survival.

After living in the wilderness for such a long time, Yoshkar Ola looked and felt like a city, but it was far from being one. At the most it was a small town, but since it was the capital of Mari-El Autonomous Republic, it held offices of the government, Party headquarters, and the Ministry of Agriculture. There was also a hospital, a school, and a post office, as well as an assembly hall mainly used for Party meetings. Occasionally, there would be a film shown there for the public.

I had no difficulties in adjusting to life here. The chores around the house remained almost the same. In the morning, the stove had to be lit, for which wood had to be brought in. Water had to be carried from the well. Potatoes had to be peeled and cooked, although still in water without salt. After bread and hot water for breakfast, I looked after our animals and let them graze outside or on the street. With the warm weather and exposure to the sun, my fingers started to heal and my body bounced back to normal. I never grew even an inch taller, though, and many of my teeth were gone.

Once again, we did the best to make our apartment suitable for living. I scrubbed the floor with an old piece of metal to remove dirt, then rinsed it with water and an old rag. I used the water sparingly so I wouldn't have to carry so many buckets from the well, and I threw the dirty water on the grass outside the house. We cleaned the windows, or what was left of them, since broken glass had been replaced with wood. I found a broken bottle, which I filled with water and decorated with flowers I picked in the fields. I put this floral arrangement on the table. The mound of straw that served as our bed was neatly piled in one corner. The kitchen was used by all four families, which sometimes resulted in quarrels over the usage of the stove. Every week, one family had to scrub the kitchen floor and as a reward would be the first to use it. Once a month it was my responsibility to do this. Every family had their own wood.

Each family kept to themselves, no one trusted a neighbor, and we didn't have lengthy conversations with anyone. We were all afraid that anyone could be a spy ready to inform the Party of someone's activities and beliefs. We kept to ourselves, and even within the four walls of our room we spoke in whispers so no one could hear us. We were all concerned about the NKVD watching us. In this respect, I missed the freedom of kolkhoz life, where the peasants were much friendlier and only the trees and animals could hear what we said. I missed the forest that provided us with berries, mushrooms, and edible weeds.

I was sorry for my animals, too. One day our goats disappeared. We were informed that they had been arrested by the militia for grazing on the street and had been taken to the city corral. Mother went to claim them, but when she got there, she found dozens of goats that all looked alike. Fortunately, our goat recognized Mother's voice and ran to her. She was then told that after paying a bail of a hundred rubles she could take her goats home, but she was sternly warned that the next time bail would be five times larger. Unable to feed so many goats, we were forced to sell the two kids. This loss ended our hope of having milk. We were left with our rations of food consisting of some potatoes and three slices of bread per day. Pig had to be very hungry, like the rest of us.

Summer was almost over. The situation on the front changed after the German defeat in Stalingrad and the Soviet army was slowly advancing, giving us all hopes for the day when war would end. Unexpectedly a letter from Kazik arrived, finding us at our new address after a long journey. Mother wouldn't let go of the letter and held it tightly in her hands. We read it over and over again, finding meaning in each word. He informed us that he was fine and was heading in the direction of Berlin. Our happiness over Kazik's letter was dimmed by the fact that it was written many weeks ago.

With the passing of the short summer, which was chased away by cold winds and gray clouds covering the warm sun, it was time for me to enroll in school. The school building was a strong wooden structure, not too far from home. I met some of the teachers and students, few of whom were native to the area. Mostly they were also refugees from cities occupied by Nazis in the Ukraine or from the cities of Moscow and Leningrad. After the little cabin school in Toryal, this school seemed like a big one to me. There were many classrooms, halls, and an auditorium, but for some reason I didn't feel comfortable.

In September classes began. I put on my worn-out winter clothes and patched *valenki* and went to school. I was glad that I didn't have to walk in the forest and be gone from my parents for five days, and very happy that I'd be with my parents instead of strangers during the long nights. After walking just a few blocks, I arrived at school knowing that I'd be home in the afternoon.

After just one day, however, I realized how difficult it was going to be for me. Most of the students came from good backgrounds in big cities, and they spoke perfect Russian. The teachers were the same. In the farm school at Toryal, my foreign accent had not been noticed. Once again I was labeled as a foreigner, *polachka*. This same belittling term, which a completely different group of children had also called me, was very hard for me to bear. Adding to this insult, all of the students were much better dressed than I was because they had been able to leave their homes in a more orderly manner. Now I was a refugee again. The students looked down on me harshly and left me to myself. Even worse, these teachers held the same attitude that I could not possibly know more or be more articulate than Russian students. One teacher, however, our military instructor, liked me. He often praised my knowledge of arms and the mechanics of military vehicles. We still had a shortage of paper to contend with, but we had access to more books. I had no difficulty keeping up with my class in geography, literature, chemistry, or physics. The German language, however, caused me problems. It was required, and I detested it.

I learned to be very good in the class of Marxism-Leninism, which was the principal structure of our Communist education. We were instructed in the superiority of socialism and were taught that religion was the opium of the proletariat, or working classes. Our beloved Father Stalin—with his infinite knowledge, goodness, and genius for leadership—was supposedly bringing us victory over the Germans and the capitalist world. Without realizing it, I started to believe this myself until an innocent incident occurred with one of my classmates.

One of the girls in my class was from Odessa (now Odesa), and she was also Jewish. I became more friendly with her than any other girl. On a few occasions, I was even invited to her home. I met her mother, her father, who was in the army, and her older sister, who was a member of the Communist Party. Then one day I invited her to my home. A couple of days later, as we were walking from school, she suddenly turned to me and asked, "Tell me the truth. What was your father in Poland? His hands don't look like the hands of a working-class person."

At first my heart stopped. Then it accelerated until I felt pulsations in my head and throughout my whole body. I had the good sense to control myself and in a matter-of-fact voice answered her without hesitation. "But what a silly question," I told her. "Of course

In Yoshkar Ola, 1944, Hanna (right) and the girl who asked, "What was your father in Poland?"

he was a worker, a bookkeeper for some factory in Łódź. Would we be here, in Russia, if it was otherwise?" My quick and seemingly calm answer was convincing, because she never asked again.

That evening when I came home and we sat down to our dinner of boiled potatoes served in our single bowl, I described this episode to my parents. No sooner had I finished telling about it than Father's spoon dropped from his hands, spilling precious food, and Mother's spoon fell, too. She turned white. They got up and talked briefly together. I was terribly frightened. "Your friend's questions could have serious consequences," Father said. "Her sister is a member of the Communist Party and is employed in a high position. She could inform the NKVD of any suspicions she has about my background. The safest thing for me to do is to go into hiding for a few days." Without finishing his evening meal, Father picked up his coat and left the house. I was not told where he was hiding. It was better for me not to know in case of an NKVD intervention and interrogation. His absence from work was justified by informing the office that he was ill.

The next day I had to go to school with a happy face and pretend it was an ordinary day for me. Only at night, when Mother and I were alone, could we be ourselves and share our worry and anxiety, crying in each other's arms. Luckily, no one came or made inquiries about us.

After a few uneventful days, Father returned home and we resumed our normal schedule. We realized how fragile our future in the Soviet Union was, however, and how easily our lives could be destroyed. After all we'd been through to survive these terrible years, and with no end of the war in sight, we were still in danger. For us, the only hope was to escape from Russia. At that time, though, this feat was as impossible as transforming night into day. We had to continue walking our tightrope and patiently wait to see what the future and destiny would bring.

The full brunt of winter hit us again and brought continuing struggles for warmth and food. Poor Pig was in sad shape by now. He was full grown but very skinny. He was always hungry because there was not enough food to feed him. My parents and I didn't discuss him. One day I was very surprised when I came home from school because of the commotion in our house. I was met by Mother, who stopped me at the door and started to talk to me, but I saw meat in the kitchen. She didn't have to explain or say anything to me. I understood in seconds what had happened. No sooner had I left for school than the butcher was called. For some amount of payment, my friend and pet was butchered. My sadness had no limit, nor did my anger. At first I refused to eat my meal. The soup with potatoes and a few pieces of pork looked so wonderful, however. A little island of fat floating in it brought memories of a forgotten flavor. This taste was too much to resist. Even without salt, we had a feast, our first one in years. I ate my soup to the last drop.

There was plenty of ice outside, so the meat was frozen. Throughout that winter we had some meat, which we stretched to the maximum. Nothing was wasted and the bones were cooked over and over again. The matter of survival between Pig and us brought no hesitation over who had to be sacrificed.

Although we lived in a bigger town, it was still primitive. One of the biggest problems was the outhouse. There was one outhouse for the four apartments, in which fourteen persons lived. The little wooden hut contained a big hole on top of which was a wooden bench with a round opening in the middle. During the winter months, human waste would freeze. With so many people using it, the hole below would fill up and reach the bench. It was impossible to clean this mess. It formed a repulsive, solid icy heap which covered the opening of the bench. The only way to clean it was to chip the mess with an ax, but nobody was willing to do it. Consequently, we were forced to relieve ourselves behind the hut. This caused many unpleasant and embarrassing situations. I missed our forest with its many trees and leaves and solitude. Yes, leaves, for paper was unobtainable.

There was also the problem of bathing, with one bathhouse in which to shower. It was opened only one day a week. Tickets for the bathhouse had to be secured ahead of time. It had two rooms— one for men, the other for women. The floor was cold stone, filthy with mud. It was very cold inside, since the doors were constantly opened by people going in and out.

Each room was called a sauna and had benches in the middle and cabinets on the wall. Women in attendance brought each person a tin basin, sometimes with holes in it patched with dirty rags, and a tiny piece of soap of undeterminable color or smell. The lucky persons had a place on one of the benches. If not, there was a waiting line for a place.

Once we had obtained a place on the bench, there was another line for hot water. Then, with our basin filled with hot water, it was time for a bath. The tiny piece of soap was barely enough to wash our hair, but we gained experience in stretching it to wash our entire bodies. We only had one chance to rinse ourselves, as being in line for another basin of water was not appealing. Also, it was very cold, and any empty place on the bench was quickly occupied. After a bath, we dressed and ran home. More than once, warm water was used up by the time it was our turn and we had only cold water in which to bathe. No more water could be heated because of the lack of wood.

And so another year went by. It was almost five years since the war had started, and there was still no end in sight. The Russian army was advancing, and by the end of 1943 and the beginning of 1944 the German army was in retreat. Moscow was out of danger. Kiev,

Odessa, Leningrad, and other cities in the Ukraine and Byelorussia were liberated. Each victory over the Germans was applauded and celebrated. There was no family in Russia that didn't have someone on the front lines. Fathers, brothers, sons—all were fighting and losing their lives to defend this country. The eyes of mothers, wives, and sisters were filled with tears. This sadness included our family, too, because we hadn't had any news from Kazik.

In the routine of our daily existence, unexpected incidents sometimes occurred. One night we heard Mother scream, and we all jumped out of our straw bed. We were on our feet in seconds, and Father turned on some light. Right there in the middle of the room lay a big, gray, repulsive rat. In her sleep, Mother felt something crawling on her chest and instinctively she reached with her hand and grabbed the tail of the rat. When she screamed, she threw it with full force and the rat was killed by the impact. Father picked up the dead rat by the tail and went outside to throw it out. To our relief, Mother was not scratched or bitten. For many nights after that, we were alert to any noise or squeak in our room. But even this we eventually got used to. We never had another incident like this one, but we noticed that our sack of flour started to have holes. We couldn't afford to lose this treasure, so at night we lifted the heavy sack to store it on the table.

Schools in Russia didn't have divisions. There was just one school, which started with first grade and ended in tenth. A student had ten years of schooling, after which one either entered higher education or vocational school or was sent to assigned work. Education was free, even at the university level, but everything was based on grades. Bad students didn't have a chance for further education unless they were children of high-ranking Party leaders. Then there were no restrictions.

I was approaching the end of my schooling, and we began to consider the alternatives for my future. We were afraid that I would be drafted to a vocational school or sent to work in a Russian factory because factory workers were badly needed. In this case, I would be separated from my parents and would become the property of the state. I would be under strict orders from the government about where to work, what kind of work to do, and where to live. Dreams of my ever returning to Poland would vanish.

Hanna (front right) with her tenth grade class, in the last year of school in Yoshkar Ola.

I desperately started looking for higher education. My first choice was Moscow, which was out of danger now. My uncles and aunts and their families had already returned to their homes. Before they left for Moscow, Father had obtained a special assignment to travel for business. For this designation he needed a *komandirovka* (travel permit). With great difficulty and special bribes, he was able to get it. He packed a loaf of bread and went to Sverdlovsk. His actual reason for taking this trip was to see his mother before she returned to Moscow. He met with his family and had a tearful reunion. This reunion didn't attract any particular attention at this time because so many refugees were traveling to return home. From his family, Father learned that his sister's youngest son, an eighteen-year-old, had been killed in battle, and that his other nephews were still on the battle front. They talked all night, and in the morning he said goodbye to all of them. Soon after this trip, his family returned to Moscow. We hoped I could get placed in school there, and I filled in many forms and applications to any possible schools. Then I waited for the answers.

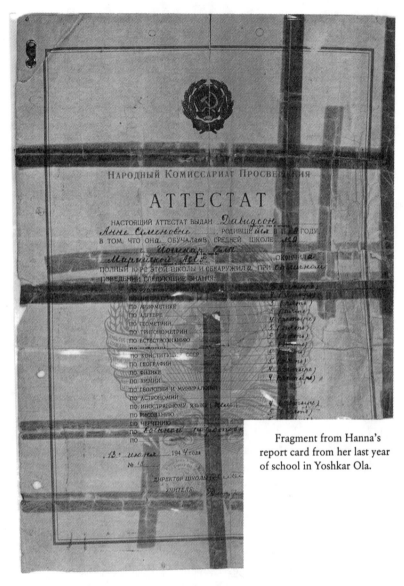

Fragment from Hanna's report card from her last year of school in Yoshkar Ola.

Meanwhile our school was almost over. I passed final examinations with honors in spite of the difficulties from teachers. All of my classmates were returning to their homes in liberated cities, including the girl from Odessa. We were the only family with no place to go.

It was very difficult to be accepted in the Moscow schools, and I was rejected by all but one. This was the School of Metallurgic Engineering, and engineers from this school were in high demand. While this profession was not to my liking, I had no choice but to accept. At least I would be safe with family in Moscow.

The last day of school was celebrated by taking class pictures, speeches, and farewells. This procedure didn't upset me because I was glad to leave this school. There was a noticeable absence of boys, however, which was very sad. They all had been drafted for training and preparation to be sent to the front lines to replace an endless amount of wounded or dead soldiers.

During the summer, I received an acknowledgment of acceptance to school, which was necessary for me to obtain a permit to travel; a date for my entrance examination; and applications for assignments in dorms and a cafeteria. I was ready to go to Moscow, but I was not too sure about going alone. I knew I would not see my parents until the end of the school year. Yoshkar Ola was very far from Moscow, and trains didn't run too often. When they did, they were filled to capacity, frequently packing standing passengers tightly together. It was terribly difficult to purchase a ticket. As much as I wanted to stay home with my parents, I knew I would not be permitted to do so.

There was not too much to be done to prepare for my trip. The biggest problem was obtaining a *komandirovka*. I went to the Department of Education and presented my acceptance to school. There I had to fill in questionnaire after questionnaire with information about my parents, grandparents, brother, uncles, and aunts. I became a master in providing the proper answers. From the beginning, I'd learned that to save ourselves we had to hide under false statements.

My parents didn't want to let me go on my own because this was a very difficult and complicated trip. Father wanted to accompany me, and he obtained permission to travel from Narkom, the Ministry of Agriculture. To travel to Moscow required a confirmation from the NKVD, however, and they absolutely refused. With Father's luck and mine, at the last minute the rules for travel were softened a little. On the pretense that he had a mission for Sovnarkom in Moscow, his permission was granted.

Hanna's 1945 permit from her Moscow school for traveling during vacations.

The day approached when I had to pack my few belongings. I put them in a sack tied with rope, just as I did in Kuzhnur, and I was ready. Father had even less luggage. We dried some bread to have food on the trip and packed it in a small sack. Only after packing did I realize that I was leaving the safety of my nest and that I'd be flying on my own wings for a very long time.

"You'll see different places," Mother told me that last night. "You'll be in Moscow, the capital of Russia, with theaters, museums, concerts, the opera. It is good for you to learn more of life besides the forest and the farm."

"I know," I replied. "But I don't want to be alone. I want you and Father to go with me."

"This is impossible," she said. "You understand this. We will miss you terribly, but you have to go alone. We cannot go with you." We both cried a long time. The excitement of seeing new things was great, but the separation from my family was very painful. Mother, who had no knowledge of the fate of her first child, must now send her second child to a new life, alone.

When morning came, we left home. Mother accompanied us to the train station. The train was already there, and we had to board. I remember my mother standing on the platform alone, waving to me as I sent kisses to her with my hand. As the train pulled out of the station, I leaned out of the window and watched her grow farther and farther away from me until all I could see was a tiny dot in the distance. And then, even this tiny dot was gone.

From Yoshkar Ola to Kazan, the ride was easy. In Kazan, we transferred to the Moscow train. The minute we stepped off the first train, we were swallowed by a mob of travelers and refugees returning to Moscow. We waited for a long time before the train for Moscow arrived, and when it finally pulled up to the platform, the crowd stormed the boxcars. I stayed close to Father, holding his hand with all my might in terror that we'd be separated or crushed to death. As we reached the door, Father jumped on the boxcar ledge and pulled me in, squeezing me inside and protecting me from behind. Somehow we both managed to get inside and even grabbed one space on a bench, which we shared. At least we were in. We stayed in the station all night. In the middle of this long night, two NKVD agents entered the train, checking everyone's documents. When our turn came, they approved my permit but detained Father's and took him for further investigation. Stricken with panic, I sat on the dark train not knowing what to do or who to ask for advice. No one wanted to risk being seen talking to a relative of a man taken away by the NKVD. People were afraid even to look at me.

After an hour passed and Father had not returned, I memorized my grandmother's address and destroyed the slip of paper on which it was written. I was afraid that since Father was detained, I would be asked questions, too. It was impossible to predict what an NKVD man with a little power might do, and I couldn't jeopardize the lives of our family in Moscow. When another hour passed, I was in despair and expected the worst. I couldn't believe that this simple trip to school would end in the destruction of our family. For five years, I'd been told how lucky I was to be in a socialist country. For five years, I was filled with ideas of my freedom and the equality of all people. For five years, I was assured of the righteousness of our beloved Stalin. For five years, I was told that children were not responsible for the actions of our parents. Yet here I was, sitting on a train that would take me to continue my education and my family could be destroyed for no reason at all. I couldn't understand this. My whole mind and body were rigid with fear, and I was terrified for Father.

At the end of the third hour, I felt someone approaching. In the darkness, I couldn't identify who was coming. My heart beat as though it would burst, and I held my breath. "Hanna. I am back." I jumped into Father's arms and only then did I allow myself to burst into uncontrollable sobbing. Father told me he'd spent equally miserable hours awaiting the unpredictable verdict from a drunken NKVD man, terrified about what was happening to me. With no explanation, probably because they could not find an irregularity in Father's papers, they let him go. We never did know why they decided to remove him from the train in the first place. In the morning, the train pulled out of the station at Kazan and began taking us to Moscow. Father and I were calmed down by now, and the slow motion and monotonous sound of the wheels lulled us. We dozed, leaning closely next to each other on our crowded seats. When I opened my eyes, we were already traveling west at full speed, which was not very fast. With every turn of the wheel, I was getting farther and farther away from forests, mountains, farms, and the peacefulness of the remote countryside. With every minute passing, I was closer and closer to a different life.

Our supply of dry bread was running low, so we ate very slowly, stretching the piece of bread as much as possible. In some stations, we could find some hot water, which helped us chew the bread. At each of the many stations where we stopped, large crowds stormed the train trying to get on. Few people got off. We didn't dare get up and stretch ourselves for fear that if we moved, our seat would be taken away, which would mean we'd have to travel standing up, stepping over exhausted travelers sitting on the floors, mostly children or older people. Bathrooms were impossible to reach. Father and I would take turns running out of the train at a station to relieve ourselves behind the train.

As hours went by, I could see the villages become bigger and more frequent. The landscape changed, and there were more open spaces and cultivated farmland. The next morning, we approached the outskirts of Moscow. My excitement grew with each minute, and I left my seat and pushed my way to a window. Small houses were gradually replaced with bigger buildings, sparsely traveled roads turned into streets filled with typical city traffic. The train slowed its speed, and for the first time I saw the skyline of Moscow.

9
A YEAR IN MOSCOW

I don't know what I expected, but I was disappointed. Accustomed to green forests and open spaces, I found the gray, huge, confining buildings overwhelming. I was aware of mixed feelings of excitement, expectation, and disillusionment. Finally the conductor announced, "Moscow." The whistle blew, and the train stopped. A crush of exhausted people started rushing to the exits, and Father held me tightly so I wouldn't be hurt or separated from him. We had plenty of time. Moscow lay before us.

We picked up our small sacks and held them on our backs. Then we left the train and the station. I found myself on a very busy street with mostly pedestrians and military men who were walking. There were just a few cars passing by, but there were many buses and electric trains. My head was spinning with the noise of the big city and the sight of the sidewalks between the huge buildings. I gasped for air because I felt suffocated. I'd forgotten everything about living in the city after so many years of living in the country. I remember that my feet hurt. I was used to walking barefooted on soft ground and grass, and now I was wearing someone's old boots, which were new to me. Father had obtained these boots for me on the black market in Yoshkar Ola. Still, I was very drawn to this artery of life with so much movement, so much noise, and so many people. I was ready for new experiences and a new life.

Father knew Moscow well, and it was easy for him to find his sister Zina's house. Aunt Zina lived with her husband Abraham and her daughter Iza, in an apartment on the second floor. Like all other apartments that had belonged to one family before the revolution, hers was now occupied by several families. This three-room apartment housed three families who shared one kitchen and one toilet.

We arrived at Aunt Zina's home late in the morning. Everyone was at work except Iza, who was a year older than I and was on vacation from school. We were glad that none of the neighbors were at home, because we were afraid someone might recognize Father from the time he lived in Moscow. There was always the possibility that someone would denounce us to the NKVD. After talking with Iza, it was decided that I would be introduced as Uncle Abraham's distant relative who was sent to school in Moscow. With no rest, Father left the apartment and went to the post office where Zina worked. They said a tearful hello, pretending to be old friends; then he left to see the rest of the family.

As he passed by one of the government stores, he spotted cigarettes and ventured in to buy one, which was a real luxury. As he was paying, he heard someone tapping on the counter. As he turned around, he saw a woman. Even after twenty years, they recognized each other. They began to talk, pretending to be very casual, when the woman's sister walked in. "Go away quickly," his friend said. "My brother-in-law is a dangerous NKVD member." With no goodbyes, Father picked up his cigarette and walked out. Even this small purchase could have turned into a tragedy for us.

The obligation of a traveler was that upon arriving at a destination, one had to report to the military and register the passport. Father wanted to stay in Moscow for a few days, so he didn't report his passport for a day or two. He decided he could always blame the train for his delay in arriving. He stayed with Aunt Zina for a few nights, sneaking in after dark and leaving very early in the mornings to see the rest of his family.

In order to live in Moscow, I had to show my passport as well as my permission from the school to the authorities, and I had to register in my dorm. Iza gave me directions, explaining how to get there and which bus to take. With my documents and my small bundle on my back, I left their apartment. Once on the street alone, my heart began to beat with accelerating speed. I had to stand there for a minute to collect my courage. There was nothing else to do, so I proceeded by myself.

I followed instructions and found the correct bus station. I asked if the bus would take me to my destination, and the bus driver said she knew the dorms well and promised to tell me where to get off.

Her bus was terribly overcrowded. Everyone was pushing to get on or off. I managed to stay close to the front just in case the driver forgot me and saw for myself the distinguished dorm building.

I wasn't forgotten. The bus driver stopped at the right place, and I pushed myself out of the bus. I went to the office and was directed to the proper authority. I wasn't the only one there. Lots of old and new students crowded the waiting room. I took my number and patiently waited for my turn to come. I was finally admitted to the office and assigned to sit behind one of many desks. Once again, I had to fill in answers on questionnaires, endless questions about my past and relatives. Then another clerk asked me the same questions, but I had to answer verbally rather than writing this time, in order to check and see if my answers corresponded with what I'd written. I felt like I was being interrogated for a crime instead of being admitted as a student.

In the end, I was accepted. I was given tickets to the cafeteria, tickets for linens and a pillow, tickets for a bed, and tickets for my room. With all these tickets, I went from one place to another to collect my treasures. I followed instructions to my building and found that my room was on the third floor. I climbed the stairs and then entered a very long, dark corridor with doors on both sides. I found my room number and opened the door. Five girls were already there. No one asked me any questions or paid any attention to my entrance. They were preoccupied with themselves.

The room was small and long, with one window in the middle of the smallest wall. There were six narrow metal beds, three in a row on each wall with a space between them. The best beds closer to the windows were taken, so I took the last one next to the door. The room was in sorry shape with white paint peeling from the walls, a dirty concrete floor, and a small window to the outside that gave little light. One electric bulb hung from a cord. There were no tables or desks. The look of it all was so depressing that I had to use all my willpower to keep from crying. I saw that one's possessions were kept under the bed, including books, and learned that homework was done in the library.

I made my bed with a blanket and linens of indeterminate color, sort of grayish and very rough. Remembering the open spaces in Kuzhnur and feeling very much alone, I felt terribly confined in this small, dark room. It was about mealtime, and we all went to the cafeteria where, with our ticket, we were each given a bowl, spoon, fork, and knife for the duration of the semester, and stamps for our meals. The appearance of the cafeteria matched the rest of the rooms in the building, and this first meal was not much better. We had a watery soup with some potatoes and a few leaves of cabbage and a slice of bread. The soup had salt in it, however! Moscow apparently had a better supply of food.

After the meal there was nothing to do, so I asked the supervisor for permission to leave for the afternoon and to spend the night with friends. Fortunately, this permission was granted. I decided to explore the city a little on my own and then return to Aunt Zina's home. Father came later and we spent the night with the family, talking in whispers so the neighbors would not hear us. I slept with Iza and Father slept on the floor.

Early the next morning I had to take an entrance examination, and Father went to the school with me. New students from all over Russia were crowded there, and we were directed to the auditorium in which tests were held. A girl my age was walking on one side of me and started talking. "If I don't pass these exams," she said, "I will be returned home and my parents will never forgive me." Her name was Nela. She was from Leningrad and was the daughter of a very high-ranking military man. She'd been sent to Moscow to her

Nela, Hanna's new friend in Moscow, 1945.

uncle, a very high Party official attached to the Kremlin who was in direct contact with Stalin himself.

At that time I didn't know her at all, not even her name, but I tried to reassure her. "Sit by me and I'll help you," I told her. "I'll write the answers slowly and with the biggest letters I can. You can give me a signal when I can turn the page."

We were separated by one empty seat, but she could see. The exams were easy and I had no difficulties, but I went very slowly so Nela could copy my answers. I was almost the last one to leave the room. Father was waiting for me with anxious expectation thinking I was having problems with the exams, which would mean for me to return to Yoshkar Ola to be drafted by the government to work at a factory somewhere in Russia. I laughed and explained to him what happened. We left school quickly because we didn't want Nela to see Father with me, just as a precaution.

Nela and I both passed the exams with flying colors and were both accepted in school. She was happy for passing the tests, and I was equally happy for having a new friend.

Father stayed in Moscow for a few days more, visiting his mother and brother and sister and their families, all the while hiding from neighbors. Then he left to return to Yoshkar Ola and I started the routine of school life in earnest. Aunt Zina didn't want me to stay with them too often because she was afraid of the neighbors. I stayed in the dorms, but I frequently visited my grandmother and Fania, Father's younger sister.

On the first day of school, I met Nela outside. We walked to class together, which gave me the security of a companion, and we found that we would be attending all our classes together. We had classes from eight in the morning till two in the afternoon, after which we had to attend the library to do homework. We couldn't choose subjects. All of us had to take the curriculum dictated by the school. We took math, history, geography, Russian, and a foreign language (I took English). There was special emphasis on chemistry, physics, and Marxism-Leninism, which was drilled into us; any student who failed the latter faced an end to further education. Good grades were required. Without them, after three failures, a student was expelled from school. Education was free (including books, supplies, dorms, and the cafeterias), so the pressure for good grades was high.

I was placed in a program to become a metallurgist, and while I didn't like my future profession, I had no choice at all in the matter. I did very well at school and continued to help Nela. Our most difficult subject was mechanical drawing, which required accuracy, neatness, concentration, and time. Sometimes we had to work late into the evening, even then not accomplishing perfect work. We took our meals in the cafeteria, and then Nela would go home after school and I went to the dorm. This place was a source of much unhappiness for me. Life in the dorms was difficult. Sharing such a small space among six girls brought on many squabbles. What was even worse was sharing one bathroom at the end of the corridor with dozens of girls, with no privacy for toilets. The cafeteria was bad, too, because of the long lines we stood in to obtain miserable food and a slice of bread.

"You cannot stay there," Fania told me one day. "Come and live with us."

I jumped at this invitation and moved in right away. Officially I couldn't leave the dorms. I didn't have permission to be any other place. So I would sleep in the dorms once in awhile and punch my cafeteria tickets. My roommates didn't object to having one person less in the room, but I had to be very careful not to be denounced to authorities because of my frequent absences.

Fania, her husband Marc, and I became very close. They didn't have any children and were delighted to have me with them. I looked very much like Fania and could easily have been taken for her daughter, which presented a big problem. Fania, Marc, and Grandmother Raquel occupied one room, sharing their apartment with two other families. My family had been in this apartment ever since the revolution, when my father was still living with them. At that time, Fania was not yet married. After Father left Russia, Aunt Fania got married and her husband moved into the same room, since it was almost impossible to obtain a new apartment. When Father escaped from Russia to Poland, neighbors were given the explanation that he didn't survive an illness, and his existence was forgotten.

When I moved in with them, curious neighbors were told that I was a distant relative of Uncle Marc's, visiting for a short time. I was illegally in their apartment. I resembled Fania instead of Uncle Marc. Therefore, I was actually a criminal. Since one of the neighbors worked for the NKVD and was suspicious about everything, we had to be extra careful. I would never leave the room before Fania checked whether anyone was in the kitchen or the hall. Coming back was easier, because every family had its own code of knocking for admittance. If someone was watching, Fania would open the door and signal me to go away. She must have loved me very much to take these tremendous chances.

The apartment was furnished with a sofa bed on one wall next to the window. This is where Fania and Marc slept. There was a large wardrobe that stood in the middle of a wall, which was used for storing clothing and linen. On one side of this wardrobe was a bed for Grandmother against the wall. She had a screen that she extended during the night for privacy. Against another wall was a sofa, where I slept, and in the center of the room were a table and chairs.

Moving in with family changed my entire life in Moscow. The luxury of sleeping on the soft sofa with clean linens and a real feather pillow made me feel like royalty. What a wonderful time it was! The warmth of the family, their loving care, and the better food were the best ingredients for existence. I hated the nights when I had to go to the dorms!

Staples were more plentiful in Moscow; we even had some sugar. We were still limited to strict food rations, though. Since only Fania, Marc, and Grandmother were entitled to a ration of food, I ate some of my meals in the cafeteria.

Trading for goods on the black market brought severe punishment, sometimes death, but the black market flourished anyway. At times Fania or Marc would go to this market and buy vegetables, more grain, or extra bread.

I helped Fania as much as I could doing chores, but only within the four walls of our room. I helped in the kitchen only when we were sure that no one was at home and used the toilet only when Fania had checked that no one was in the hall. We established a routine and got used to it. Not one of the neighbors was aware of me living in Fania's room, and only once did I encounter one of the neighbor women. Unaware that someone was home, I went to the kitchen. She entered the kitchen and I quickly turned my head after a short hello and returned to our room. Fania told her later that Marc's relative came for tea. We never made a mistake like this again.

Every morning I was up before anyone else to use the toilet and wash my face. After a short breakfast of bread and tea, I would leave quietly and go to school. I worked hard and enjoyed learning, especially reading. For the first time I had access to books and I devoured them. I memorized Pushkin's poetry. I couldn't put down Dostoevsky, Tolstoy, Lermontov, Gogol, and others. Mostly I read Russian authors because foreign books were scarce.

Nela and I became inseparable. Realizing how beautiful Moscow was, we explored the city together. There was so much to see. We went to museums, even though exhibits were few because works of art had been stored and evacuated during the siege to protect them. We rode all the Moscow metros, which had spectacular stations with beautiful architecture. We became familiar with parks, Red Square, and interesting buildings. I wasn't afraid anymore and had quickly adapted myself from the remote forest to a bustling city. I had a friend now, a loving family, and what felt to me like a loving home.

I was able to keep Nela separate from my family by not inviting her to our home and never revealing my past to her. As far as she knew, I came from Yoshkar Ola, and I had remote family who occasionally invited me to stay with them. She knew I lived in the dorms. I had learned well how to tell the story of myself, omitting dangerous passages and adding convenient ones. I was sorry that even with my friend I couldn't be entirely truthful and sincere, however. To avoid explanations of my frequent absence from the dorms, I invented a boyfriend and named him Misha. He lived in Moscow after being wounded on the front, and naturally I had to be with him. He became so real to me that I almost felt his presence and had long conversations with him when I was alone. Nela believed me. Sometime later she found a boyfriend, too. She never met mine and I never met hers. Maybe she was dreaming the same way I was.

Once or twice, Nela invited me to her home. I went reluctantly because I didn't want to be seen by a very high government official and have to answer inevitable questions. Her family lived in a special complex for high Party members and had a security entrance. Their apartment was big: four bedrooms for just her family of four, a dining room, living room, and their own kitchen and fully equipped bathroom. I was tempted to ask permission to take a shower there, but I was too afraid of doing so. A bathroom! I'd forgotten they existed.

I did enjoy tremendously savoring the cookies Nela offered to me. Communist leaders certainly led different lives from the rest of us. Never mind that we all memorized the fact that in socialist Russia all people are equal, with equal rights and possibilities. Only at home with Marc, Fania, and Grandmother could I express my feelings and discuss with them the realities and events of the day. This sharing we did over our watery soup, slices of bread, and hot tea.

To celebrate Russian victories over the Germans, twenty-one-gun salutes were fired during the evenings with festive and impressive fireworks. Cities liberated were called over loudspeakers installed in streets. With each victory our hearts rejoiced, knowing that these victories brought us closer to the end of the war.

The sixth winter was approaching. Moscow was far from Yoszkar Ola and the winters were not as cruel, but cold and freezing weather is very difficult everywhere. I walked on busy streets and rode buses and electric trains or metros instead of walking through a deserted forest afraid of wolves. At home, I had electric light instead of darkness, and an inside toilet instead of freezing air under a tree.

Fania, anxious to expose me to culture, would find tickets to the theater, opera, and ballet, sometimes buying them on the forbidden black market. I was drunk with the effect these events had on me. I saw *Swan Lake* in the Bolshoi Theater, with the wonderful music, costumes, scenery, and the magnificent performance itself. I saw *Scheherazade*, concerts, and dramas. I absorbed all this like a dry sponge, not ever having enough. While I missed my parents very much, I was glad to be in Moscow.

Every five days we had a day off. On those days Fania and I visited our relatives. Aunt Zina never invited me to her house, and I didn't see my cousin Iza unless she was visiting her grandma. I met Aunt Sima, Father's older sister, and her husband, and shared with them their tragedy of losing their eighteen-year-old son, Pablo, and having Igor, their oldest son, still in battle. I met my Uncle David, Father's oldest brother, and Aunt Lisa and cousin Lusia, who was a year or two older than I. I also met other more distant relatives. Not one of them, however, was happy having me in their homes. I was a stranger, and fear of having a stranger in their apartment, or rather room, was very strong. It was a fact of life that anyone—a neighbor, a friend, even a relative—could denounce and inform the NKVD that an unknown person was their visitor, and this situation was always dangerous. Only Lusia frequently visited Fania and Grandmother.

This constant fear of being exposed was the dark side of my living in Moscow. Neighbors didn't trust each other; relatives would talk among themselves quietly, feeling that someone might be listening and inform authorities. There was constant suspicion, fear, and apprehension. Every word was weighed. Every step was measured. Never did the whole family gather together. Big crowds would call too much attention.

Lusia and I got along fine, but we never became friends. She was Grandmother's favorite. I remained a stranger to Grandmother, even after living in the same room. I never knew why. Perhaps because she was so old by then. I never knew her age, but she was very close to ninety. Perhaps it was difficult for her to accept me as her granddaughter. After our evening meal of cereal, bread, and tea, I loved to comb her long silver hair and braid it. Then she would go to her corner of the room, extend the divider for privacy, and go to bed. I would sit talking with Marc and Fania or I would study. Then we would turn out the light so we could undress and go to sleep. I learned to dress in the mornings under my blanket and I tried not to look when Uncle Marc was getting dressed. We respected each other's privacy as much as we could.

Once, Grandmother got up in the middle of the night and lost her balance. We jumped out of our beds, turned on the light, and found her disoriented and obviously in distress. We did what we could to make her comfortable. Early the next morning, Fania sent me to the clinic to seek help from the doctor. When I arrived, there was already a line for emergencies. I had no choice but to wait my turn. When finally I approached the desk, I was asked what I needed. "My grandmother is very sick," I said. "Please help." Then I had to give Grandmother's name, avoiding mine.

"How old is she?" the clerk asked.

"She is more than eighty," I answered.

The clerk looked at me and laughed. "What for you want a doctor?" she said. "We don't have doctors to spare for old people." And she called the next person.

I returned home, not believing the cruelty of such behavior. Fania saw me come in alone and understood without words. It was terribly upsetting to see Grandmother helpless, knowing that we could do nothing but hold her hand. Fania took a white cloth out of the dresser. "I saved this to have something to bury her in," she said, "according to her wishes. She wants to observe the law of the Jewish religion and be draped in plain white cloth after she's dead."

We held our tears and kept our vigil until it was time for me to go back to school. Fania checked that no one was in the hall, as always, and I ran out. All day I thought of Grandmother. I expected the

Raquel Davidson (1863-1955), Hanna's paternal grandmother, in 1930.

worst and was distracted during classes. I couldn't explain why to
Nela. I just told her I didn't feel good.

When I returned home, I was afraid to knock at the door. When
Fania opened the door, one look at her smiling face lifted my spirits.
Walking into the room, I saw my grandmother sitting at the table
and eating. What a strong woman she was! Thin, petite, but strong!

We never knew what was wrong with her and we couldn't explain her recovery. What was important was that she was fine. But I couldn't understand or accept the indifference to her suffering or the denial of help for a sick person because of her age, especially here in this country where we were told that everyone had equal privileges and opportunities. I was finding out how deceptive it all was, this beautiful theory that did not apply to real life.

During this winter of 1945, Germany was cut into two fronts, with the Russians on the East and the Allies on the West, and was suffering one defeat after another. It was obvious that the Nazis were losing, and this defeat meant the end of Hitler's power.

Returning to Yoshkar Ola after his trip to Moscow, Father had a dream of eventually returning to Poland. He started to look around and had his eyes open for a possibility of getting out of this remote part of Russia and of getting closer to the Polish frontier. One day the opportunity presented itself.

The director of the bank of the Agriculture Department was trying to get transferred to the recently liberated Ukraine and organize a bank there. He needed good helpers, and Father was an excellent candidate. My parents jumped at this proposal. The plan was approved by Moscow after overcoming difficulties with Sovnarkom, the Ministry of Agriculture in Yoshkar Ola, and Father received a release from his present work with an assignment for a new job in the city of Proskurov (now Khmel'nyt'skyy).

The new bank director, knowing which strings to pull, obtained a freight car attached to the train going west. Eleven persons boarded it, with sacks of potatoes, bread, and other food available at that time. They were prepared for a very long trip, since traveling anyplace could take many weeks. Thus, a new chapter started in our lives—the beginning of our return home.

On the way to Proskurov, my parents' train passed through Moscow, where they had to wait overnight. Leaving Mother at the station, Father took this opportunity and ventured to see us. He presented himself at Fania's apartment, to her disbelief. After assuring himself that no one was in the hall, he quickly entered the room. He stayed only a short time to say a final and tearful goodbye to his mother and sister, neither of whom he ever saw again. It was a great disappointment that I was not at home. I was in the library at that time. He couldn't stay any longer and had to return to the station.

When Fania told me about his visit, I ran to the station, hopeful of seeing my parents after so many months. I searched track after track in darkness, calling their names, but there was no answer. I was desperate to see my parents, to hug them, and would not give up until I was stopped by an NKVD officer who was suspicious of my behavior and asked me my reason for being there. Without hesitation, I cried, "Ah, but I am looking for my wounded boyfriend who is supposed to be arriving in Moscow. Help me to find him!" So sincere was my outburst that he believed me, but needless to say, we could not find him. The officer said he was very sorry, maybe I would hear from him tomorrow. I took off as quickly as I could. There was no train in the station at this time, and I knew I would be interrogated to explain my presence in the station. Terribly sad, I returned home.

Again, winter was loosening its grip and spring was around the corner. This spring was different from the ones before, however. Victory and the end of the war were in the fresh warm air of spring.

On May 1, the festive day dedicated to the working people of the world, all the schools were required to take part in a parade. We gathered early in the morning with red flags, pictures of Stalin, and slogans decorated with red ribbons. We were told it was a big privilege to be marching in Red Square, with Stalin himself on the podium of the Kremlin to receive this big parade. Clouds covered the sky on this day, and rain started falling at the first light and then turned steady and cold. We stood in formation, waiting to see our beloved Father Stalin. After we had waited for two hours, our enthusiasm started to diminish. Our garments were completely soaked, and so were our feet, as we had no protection from the rain. The glorious flags and banners looked very sorry soaking wet. After three hours, we were cold, wet, and tired of standing in the rain. Yet we were not allowed to go and were forced to continue at our assigned places. After four hours, the column finally began to move. At this point, our enthusiasm had completely evaporated, but no one dared voice a complaint. Slowly, our turn came to march forward. Eventually we reached Red Square and passed in front of the Kremlin. Lots of officials were there, but Father Stalin was absent. When we finally were dismissed I ran home, wet to the bone. Fania was furious to see me in that sorry state and immediately helped me undress. She covered me with a blanket and gave me hot tea. I was lucky I didn't catch pneumonia.

One day in May, loudspeakers on the streets broke the silence announcing, "War is ended." Immediately work was interrupted. Everyone poured into the streets, crying, laughing, and singing. Six long years of struggling, suffering, losing loved ones, misery, hunger, and wandering came to an end. The mixed emotions of happiness and sorrow couldn't be separated. Neither could laughter and tears. Years of hopelessness had ended.

That night, a one-hundred-gun salute sounded in Moscow, fireworks lighted the sky with beautiful displays of colors for hours, and music filled the air from the loudspeakers. Sadness could still be seen on every face, though. There was not a single family in Russia that didn't lose at least one relative in the battles, and many were wounded.

At home with Marc and Fania and Grandmother, we talked long into the night. We didn't know the fate of our family in Poland. Neither did we have any news about Kazik. Our hearts were heavy with this sorrow.

In June, we studied for our final examination. I didn't have too much trouble with any subject except mechanical drawing, which consumed lots of time and required deep concentration. All materials such as special paper, rulers, pencils, and ink were provided. A drawing desk was available at school. It took us long hours to complete the assignment, and in the end we simply did the best we could. During the last days at school, we received our grades and said goodbye to our classmates. The majority of us had to leave Moscow. Once school was closed for the summer, we didn't have permission to reside there. Without food stamps and proper papers, there was no room for us in the city.

The last day I spent with Nela walking on the street and making plans for our futures. Nela didn't want to return to Moscow, and her plans were to continue studying in Leningrad and live with her parents. I told her that I couldn't return either and that Father had been assigned work in the Ukraine, and I would join my parents there. Then time came to say farewell. We parted as best friends, promising to write letters. She gave me her address and I promised to send her mine as soon as I joined my parents. We hugged with tears and parted.

I never sent Nela my address. I couldn't do this to her and put her safety in jeopardy. Even in her privileged position, she could be a victim of suspicion for having an association with a girl whose father was a capitalist, an enemy of the state. I often thought of her and wondered about her life and what became of her. I never knew.

10
THE JOURNEY BACK

Spring and early summer were beautiful in Moscow. I wouldn't have minded staying there longer, but it was too dangerous without permission. I had to present myself to the authorities and show my report card from school to obtain permission to travel to join my parents in Proskurov. My I.D. card showed the day of my arrival in Moscow and the day I had to leave.

I had mixed feelings about my departure. I had become very attached to Fania, Marc, and Grandmother, and I loved them dearly. They felt the same about me. Fania was very upset. She wanted so much for me to continue to live with them. While I missed my parents and couldn't wait to see them after these months, at the same time I wanted to stay in Moscow and be with Fania. But this was impossible.

I had to stay in a long line to purchase a train ticket to Proskurov. Many people traveled to liberated parts of Russia—some returning home, some assigned to new jobs, some wounded soldiers on leave to be with their families, and students like myself. At that time, trains ran on schedules but never arrived or departed on time.

When the day of my departure came, I picked up my old sack, which Fania had filled with dried bread. She managed to find some apples and a few sugar cubes for me, too. I packed my few belongings and was ready to go. I had said goodbye to Lusia and Iza and the rest of the family the day before. Now it was time to say farewell to Marc and my grandmother. I hugged her and kissed her, but I think her old mind was not ready for this separation. Grandmother made me sit down before I started the journey. She believed the superstition that this act would bring a good trip. I sat down gladly and stood up reluctantly. After our farewell, Marc left for work. Fania wanted to go with me to the station to see me off. As usual, she first checked that no one was in the hall before I walked out.

Once again, I was facing separation from family, this family I had come to love, but this time, I was leaving the familiar behind and venturing into the unknown, all by myself.

We walked to the train station. The day was pleasant, sunny, and warm, so we enjoyed our walk. We were sorry to see it end, but we couldn't stop time. We had to accept reality. Moscow Railroad Station was big and crowded. I saw luxurious trains reserved for diplomats and distinguished persons to which we, the crowd, had no access. There were some passenger trains for less distinguished people, and even these we didn't have permission to board. We searched unsuccessfully for the train that would take me to the Ukraine, and at one point we were stopped by officials so they could check our documents. I was finally directed to a freight train well out of the main building, but Fania was turned back. Somehow, after begging and explaining, they let her accompany me, much to my relief. I was afraid to go alone. I feared that I wouldn't find my train or would board the wrong one. Then I saw familiar boxcars. This train was reserved for us simple citizens.

When we approached my train, people were already boarding, even though we didn't have any idea when we'd be leaving. I found a boxcar with not too many people, and we climbed in. There were benches around the walls and a few in the middle. I found an empty one and put down my belongings. Soon two other girls arrived, and they occupied the other end of my bench. Then two young wounded soldiers came in. They took places next to us. We formed our little group of five for the duration of the trip.

I felt more secure having someone with whom to share the time, and Fania felt better, too, that I'd found some companions. It was getting late, and Fania had to return home. With much sadness we embraced and kissed and held each other. Then we said a final goodbye. Slowly she started walking home. I looked after her until she went out of sight. I felt so lonely again, and so sad, detesting this goodbye. Only the thought of seeing my parents again gave me the courage to remain on the train.

Our little group started a conversation to find out about ourselves and about our trip. Immediately our two young soldiers took it upon themselves to protect us, the girls. Late in the evening, the train started moving slowly out of Moscow. I watched as the Moscow skyline gradually disappeared into darkness. We were headed west.

That night the five of us shared our meal, mostly bread and hot water. One of the young boys was injured in a leg and an arm, but was doing reasonably well. The other boy had lost half his face. His eyebrows and eyelashes were burned off, and instead of a nose there were two holes. His left cheekbone was destroyed, and so was the left part of his lips. When I first saw him I couldn't look in his eyes. As a matter of fact, I couldn't look at him at all because I was overwhelmed by pity for him because of his horrible wounds. I was too self-conscious to face him or talk to him. During this first evening, I could see how difficult it was for him to chew the food. When complete darkness fell, we couldn't see each other anymore, but we started talking. I heard his voice when his turn came to tell his story, and he told us about the battle in which he was wounded. I stopped seeing his face and from then on I saw him as a human being just like the rest of us. I saw his pain and suffering, but I stopped pitying him. I only felt a terrible sadness that this war brought so much pain.

That night we pulled our benches together so we could stretch our legs. We left our backs to the wall and tried to sleep or at least get some rest in the noisy, crowded boxcar. When the sun rose, promising a delightful day, I opened my eyes and saw this beautiful human being who was full of hope that his face would be reasonably mended. He was full of life and plans for the future, just like all of us. I could see his coming home to a mother, who, with a broken heart, would be immensely thankful to have her son return home alive. Even today I think about him and wonder how his life turned out. During the rest of our trip, the five of us became friends, knowing that we'd never see each other again. Nevertheless, we enjoyed our companionship on this long, lonesome trip.

I remember that during one of the frequent stops, our two boys spotted an apple tree. They jumped from the train, and we saw them climbing the tree to pick some apples. Just then the train started moving again. We began yelling to them. They heard us and started to run. As they caught up with us, we extended our hands, grabbing them and finally pulling them back into the boxcar. We never let them run off again, but that day we had a delicious meal of bread and fresh, juicy apples.

We finally pulled into a small station with a wooden building that had been destroyed by bombing and shelling. All the windows were broken and there were no doors. There were only pieces of roof balancing overhead. At this point I had to change trains to the one that would take me to Proskurov. My two girl companions were to continue on the same train, but the two boys were also changing trains. I picked up my bundle and said another goodbye.

I went to the ticket window to confirm my ticket, but it was closed. A sign read, "No More Tickets—Train Full." I started looking for a conductor to give me information, but there was no one to be found. I didn't know what to do. In order to board the train, I needed my permission slip stamped. I tried to ask a few people what the procedure would be, but no one could give me an answer. They all advised me to leave as soon as possible, though, since there were gangs of Nazi admirers who raided and terrorized people. Only the past night they had stormed this station, raping or killing everyone there.

I stood helpless on the platform in a panic. Late in the afternoon a passenger train to Proskurov arrived and I ran from one wagon to another, only to be chased away because there was no room and I had no permit. At that point I became desperate. One of the soldiers jumped on the roof of a boxcar and yelled at me, "Come and jump, too." As hard as I tried, however, I couldn't jump high enough. Then the whistle blew, announcing the departure of the train. I started to cry with fright and desperation. I ran again and again, begging to be let in.

Just as the train started to move slowly on, a woman signaled to me. I ran after her boxcar and she opened the door and extended her hand. I grabbed it and she pulled me in. She was a supervisor, taking a group of girls who had been drafted to enter a vocational school. "You would be killed if you stayed there overnight," she said to me, "and I cannot permit this. Sit down and when the conductor comes asking for tickets, just raise your hand like the other girls." For the longest time I just sat sobbing in the crowded compartment, hardly believing I was in. The woman didn't talk to me again. She was busy with papers and the documents of the other girls. When the conductor came, after an hour or so of traveling, I did raise my empty hand like everybody else, and he didn't notice me. A few hours later we arrived at Proskurov.

I saw my parents first. They were looking for me. Not too many people disembarked in Proskurov, so it was very easy for us to find each other. The Proskurov station consisted of a plain wooden platform with a few railroad tracks and a crude sign board with *Proskurov* written across it by hand. I stepped down from the train, and as I ran to meet my parents I turned around and looked at the boxcar. I saw the woman, a teacher, looking at me from her window, waving and smiling. She must have been thinking that because of her, a young person was spared and given the immeasurable gift of life. I waved back, then ran to my parents.

I threw myself at my parents, so relieved to have arrived safely and to feel the protection of their arms. I had a whole school year to tell them about, and I wanted to tell them about everyone, but I was too exhausted emotionally and physically. Slowly we walked to our living quarters.

Proskurov was a small town in the Ukraine with little houses styled like those in the interior. Instead of wooden log cabins, however, they were all white—or, to be more accurate, they had been white at one time. We approached a building that was larger than the others. It was the bank in which Father was employed as a bookkeeper. The bank occupied three rooms. The fourth room was large and had a stove in the middle. This room served as an apartment for the four employees and their families. Against the walls in each of the corners stood a small, old bed for each of the families. One electric bulb hung over a rustic table with a long bench on each side.

We cooked our boiled potatoes, sharing the stove with the others, and sat down to our meal with some bread and hot water. We had a wonderful dessert of apples. The Ukraine was an agricultural state, and food was easier to obtain there.

That night I slept with my parents, sharing the only bed assigned to us. I already knew how to undress under the blanket for privacy, but to sleep, I only took off my shoes and dress. Otherwise, I slept in the same clothes that I used during the day. The last person to go to sleep would turn off the light. I had learned how to sleep with the light on when I was living in the dorm, but it was not comfortable. There was one outhouse which we all shared. Water had to be carried in from a well. At night I dreamed about Moscow, but there was a very big advantage in being in Proskurov: I was free to go in and out without fear of being seen by the neighbors.

After a few weeks of living in the back of the bank, a new clerk arrived and we had to vacate our space. Father found a two-room house, and we got permission to move into the small back room. There was no door between the rooms. One wall had a tiny window with a bed standing against the wall on each side of the window. The space between the beds was very narrow. In fact, only one person could barely stand between them. In the middle of the room was a wooden box that served as a table with a small bench on either side. In one corner was a little iron stove that smoked a lot but didn't heat the room at all. On the wall were wooden pegs on which we hung our clothes.

The front room, which was larger, was occupied by an NKVD worker and his family. We had to keep our voices down and were not able to talk freely while they were at home.

Father continued working in the bank and Mother started to work in an engineering office assisting in the department of technical drawing. I helped with the chores at home. We settled in our new home and fell into the rhythm of a different routine.

The war was over, the guns and cannon shots were silenced, Germany was defeated, and Allied and Russian armies celebrated the glorious victory. Peace in Europe was restored. Then the news of German atrocities began to reach us. We learned about the murdering of Jews and their communal graves. We lost hope of finding any of our family alive, and our days were blackened by mourning.

We saw ourselves trapped in a Communist country dominated by fear, concern, and sadness. At night, in whispers, we discussed the possibility of escaping. There was none. We decided for the time being that I would stay in Proskurov and not return to school in Moscow in case some opportunity presented itself. Neither would I go to work, using the excuse of going back to school, for fear that if I went to work and we found an opportunity, I wouldn't be released because of the desperate need for young working hands.

Then rumors reached us that the newly formed Polish government and the U.S.S.R. had formed an agreement to permit Polish citizens to return to Poland. Father jumped at this opportunity and immediately wrote a letter to the newly formed Polish Patriots

Committee, the PPC. He got an answer inviting him for a meeting in Kiev. With special permission, he was able to go. There he was nominated to be a representative of the PPC for the province of Kam'yanets'-Podil's'kyy. The first unsteady step was taken toward our return to Poland.

When Father returned to Proskurov, he obtained permission to be relieved from his duties in the bank and was assigned to work in the government office. On his desk, he placed the sign in both Russian and Polish, "Agent of the Polish Repatriation Committee" (a branch of the PPC). In his new position he received extra food rations.

At first, no one showed up. Everyone feared some kind of trap and didn't believe the authorities that repatriation was possible. Slowly, however, news got around and people began to come. Mostly they were farmers claiming Polish nationality whose sons in the Polish army fought Germans with the Russian army. All prospective repatriates were asked to give a donation to the PPC, for which they received an official receipt. Before long, they started to call my father the Polish consul.

One day while he was depositing documents, he was asked to present himself to the NKVD chief, a colonel in the Red army. Father's legs almost gave out on him as he entered the man's office. He was asked on what assumption he called himself a consul, which, the chief of NKVD said, was a misrepresentation of his function. This offense was punishable by forced labor in Siberia. Furthermore, the man wanted to know what right he had to collect a fee. Father's response was that he couldn't be responsible for what the peasants called him, and regarding the second accusation he showed papers and books with receipts that proved he had sent everything to the headquarters of the PPC. With a warning to be more careful, Father was allowed to go home. This frightened us all and convinced us even more of our need to leave Russia.

Summer was coming to an end. Once again, the trees changed colors. Green became yellows, golds, and reds, covering the woods with the magnificent splendor that came before the trees were reduced to bare brown branches. The meadows, which were full of colorful flowers during the summer, began drying and wilting. Fall approached quickly that year and was chased away by the cold northern wind. Snow fell, and winter was upon us again.

The Ukraine had a milder climate than Yoshkar Ola and the winter was not so severe, but it was still very cold, with temperatures falling below zero. I made a few friends, and we met occasionally in the home of one of the girls because her family had a little more privacy. A young Jewish couple with a baby daughter lived on the other side of Proskurov. Our families became good friends, visiting frequently. I loved to play with the baby while we spent long evenings discussing our prospects for the future. This couple had also come to Proskurov in the hope of returning to Poland. On January 1, 1946, we welcomed the New Year, which would be our seventh year of wandering, hoping that it would be our last year of exile.

In the middle of January the Soviet authorities notified Father that permission for our repatriation was granted and that we should be ready for departure. Our long-awaited dream was to become reality. We were stunned, not believing that this moment had come, not trusting the Communist Party. Thoughts emerged of the probability of a trap to put us, as undesired elements, on the train to Siberia, where we would be added to the forced-labor groups. There was nothing we could do, however, but prepare ourselves for what was to come.

That evening we went to our friends to share impressions, emotions, doubts, and hopes. We cheered each other with a glass of hot tea flavored with a piece of sugar. Later we started our walk home, enjoying the beautiful freezing winter night. The moon was shining like white diamonds on the snow that covered the silent, sleepy world around us. Suddenly two Red army officers stopped us. They were very well dressed, obviously high-ranking persons. Equally obvious to us was the fact that they were drunk beyond capacity. Seeing a nice-looking young woman on an inspiringly beautiful night triggered their romantic feelings. One of them grabbed me by the hand; the other started pushing my parents away and yelled, "Throw her on the ground."

Realizing what was happening, I began to struggle to free myself, and my parents fought, kicked, and pushed these men away from me. I managed to get free and Father shouted to me, "Run away." Which I did. I ran, completely out of breath, screaming for help. The only thing I accomplished was that the few lights on in windows were turned off. I realized with horror that there would be no help for us.

I heard the struggle going on still and turned around. The frustrated officers, seeing a horse-pulled cart, grabbed Father with the intention of throwing him under the wheel of the cart. I started to run back, but Mother screamed at me, "Run, run away." In desperation, I stood there, not knowing what to do. Then I saw one of the officers fall down, and he grabbed the other one for support. Both officers then fell down. Immediately my parents ran away, joining me. The officers were so drunk that they couldn't get up, and as we moved farther away from them we could still hear them cursing us.

Mother was hurt. She'd been hit in the eye with a fist. For many days she had a black eye. We explained her injury by saying that she had fallen and hurt her eye. In the struggle, Father lost his hat. This loss we explained by saying that a strong wind blew it away. There was no way to buy a new one. Not having a hat during the winter would expose his head to the wind, snow, and freezing rain, which would not be possible to withstand. We found an old scarf that he wore the rest of the winter to cover his head. For some time, we lived in fear that someone had seen us hitting the officers and would denounce us to the NKVD, in which case we would be sent to prison for attacking Russian military men. We couldn't wait to leave this Communist paradise.

We spent the winter speculating about our future and awaiting news of our departure. Days, weeks, and months passed by, and our morale declined. In early spring notification finally came informing all participants of our departure in one week's time. On the appointed day we were to gather at the train station to board our train.

The day we had waited for so long finally arrived, and I was sick. My cheeks were swollen and I had fever. I had contracted the mumps, unusual for one of my age. There was no point in seeing a doctor because there was no medicine available. Also, we were afraid that if our time of departure came, I would be forbidden to board the train and leave with my parents. We kept my illness a secret. I covered my head and face with a shawl when we left our room for the last time. I picked up a bag with some clothes, and another with dry bread. We were leaving Russia the same way we arrived, with nothing. We were alive, though, and that counted for more than anything.

We walked to the station, meeting other refugees on the way, and formed groups walking in the same direction. The freight train was already waiting when we arrived at the station. Our feelings were so overwhelming that we almost became numb.

An NKVD officer checked our papers. As a goodwill gesture, we were given a loaf of bread, sausage, and a pair of shoes. Then we boarded our assigned boxcar. We enjoyed the bread and sausage, but the shoes were so badly made and of such poor quality that it was not even possible to put them on, let alone walk in them. Once on the train, we were forbidden to leave. Our movements were restricted. We were informed to await further orders while the NKVD officers left with our documents, promising to be back soon.

Hours went by and no one showed up. Day was turning into dusk. Slowly the sun started disappearing on the horizon. Then it disappeared completely, submerging the earth in the darkness of the night. Still, no one showed up with our papers. Our hopes started vanishing and we were terribly afraid. The second day of waiting passed in silence. Everyone was in distress and in the same helpless situation.

On the third day, officers appeared. No one moved, expecting the worst. Surprisingly, we received our documents back, and Father was informed that permission was granted, papers were approved, and we were ready for our departure. Yet we didn't believe them. We all took our places on the floor of the boxcar, and we felt the bang of a locomotive being attached to our train. We felt a sharp pull forward and the motion of slowly turning wheels. In February of 1946, our train moved slowly from the station in Proskurov, Ukraine. Until the last minute we were not sure whether we'd be moving west toward Poland, or east toward Siberia. After a few minutes, we realized we were going in the right direction. Cold wind blowing through the open door of the freight train assured us that we were awake, not dreaming. We were, at last, on our way home to Łódź, leaving behind Russia, the Communist regime, and life under Stalin's fearsome dictatorship.

As the wheels turned faster and faster, we realized that we were really going home! The long terrible tension was broken with uncontrollable tears, hugging, cheering, and laughing. We saw telegraph poles sway in and out of sight as we watched the little houses of Proskurov disappearing in the distance. We passed villages and towns and crossed over bridges as we traveled steadily west. With each turn of the wheels, we were closer and closer to home. Orsha, Yoshkar Ola, Kuzhnur, Moscow, Proskurov, Grandmother, Fania, Marc, and my Russian family went through my mind, overshadowed by the fear of what we might find in Łódź.

NKVD officers escorted our train to the Polish border, where we got papers of our new status as repatriates. Russian rubles were exchanged for Polish money, our familiar *zloty*. The officers left the train and we crossed the border. At long last, we were back in Poland.

In the city of Katowice, we said goodbye to our fellow passengers. At that point all of us went toward a different destination. We boarded another train, this time a regular passenger train, and were seated in a compartment. We could hardly believe that we were only a few hours from Łódź! I closed my eyes trying to remember my home, but after seven years I was disappointed to find that I had forgotten many landmarks and many faces. I even had difficulty speaking Polish.

11
RETURN TO ŁÓDŹ

We passed familiar landscapes. Then suddenly, with horror, we saw in the distance the remains of a concentration camp with chimneys still black with smoke. When we asked questions about it, one man laughingly said, "This was the place where Jews were frying. Hitler did a pretty good job there." The other person in our compartment turned his head down, with silent shame in his eyes. No more words were exchanged. Was it possible that we were the only Jews traveling to Łódź?

As we reached deeper into Poland, the magnitude of the destruction became clear to us. With hearts breaking, we held hands and lowered our heads. We lost hope of finding anyone alive. What point was there in going home?

The train, with the steady rhythm of its wheels, was bringing us closer with each minute. Finally it began slowing down. We looked up to see the skyline of Łódź. We watched as the train approached, going slower and slower, until, with a final jerk, it stopped at the station so well known to us. The whistle blew, doors opened, and people started walking toward the exit. We got up from our seats, picked up our meager belongings, and followed the crowd. At the door, Father stopped for a second before descending. His face was terribly pale and his breathing was hard. He squeezed Mother's hand and I looked at her face. Her eyes were filled with tears and she could not catch her breath. I held on tightly to both of them, overwhelmed and so immensely thankful to have my parents. Carefully we descended from the train. After so many years and so many miles, we were home. But what would we find?

A typical gray February day greeted us when we stepped off the train and began our walk on a familiar street, one which we had believed we'd never see again. The city itself looked unchanged, but soon we realized it was neglected and empty. "What do we do now?" I asked. We talked and decided that first of all we would go to our home to see what was left there. We walked slowly, but as we approached our street, Bandurskiego, we accelerated our steps. Mother stumbled and almost fell, bringing to our attention the unevenness of the paving stones. As we looked down, horror overcame us. The sidewalk was paved with headstones, inscriptions well visible, of familiar names written in Yiddish and Polish. We realized these headstones were from desecrated Jewish graves. In silence, we lowered our heads and stood for awhile, tears streaming down our faces; then we stepped down from the sidewalk and continued our walk in the street.

We arrived at our apartment building and were shocked to find the same porter standing there. He immediately recognized my parents and was surprised to see us alive. He was not very friendly, but he opened the door for us and explained that our apartment was now occupied by a Polish officer. He would let us spend the night in the basement, though. He informed us coldly that we would not be allowed to see if any of our possessions had been saved. We stood in complete disbelief. Because we had no other option, Father accepted his offer. The basement was the same as it was when we left it so many years ago, except now it was dirty and very dusty. The old black sofa was still there, and Mother sat on it. Her eyes were not focused and she seemed to be lost. Without words or tears she just sat there. It was terribly hard for her to come to the happy home she'd left only to be permitted, as a beggar, to spend one night in the basement.

We settled in the basement, then ventured on the street looking for survivors. But we saw only empty houses once occupied by people we knew and loved. Finally we found a Jewish community center, where Jewish survivors could register to facilitate searching for family. We learned that my dearest friends Hania and Lilly had survived. Later we formed a small group of those who managed to come back alive.

Father and I decided to go upstairs and see our apartment. We got into the same elevator and when the door opened, we stood in front of our home. The young woman who opened the door saw two persons in old rags and wouldn't let us in. We introduced ourselves, and when she realized who we were, she started to close the door. I managed to walk into the hall, and I asked permission to check and see if any of our possessions might still be there. "No!" she shouted. "Nothing of yours is here. All is mine."

Through the open door I saw my room and saw the same lamp hanging from the ceiling. To the right, in the partially open door leading to the living room, I saw our black piano and even noticed the old white spot on the top made from a wine glass put on it during one of Kazik's parties, for which he had been in a lot of trouble. I started sobbing and ran out of there. Father came after me. "It's okay," he said, "it's okay. We are alive. Nothing else matters." This was the last time I saw my home. We never went back.

When we returned to the basement, Mother was still sitting in the same position with the same empty look in her eyes. Father couldn't face seeing her like this, so he went into the city to look around. I ventured onto the street. Without even thinking or realizing where I was going, I found myself walking in the direction of my school. As I passed my friend Ruth's home, I imagined that she was standing there waiting for me. But there was only emptiness. I continued walking four long city blocks, turned left one block, and found myself standing in front of my school. I opened the door leading to the beautiful stairway. I walked up and was in the long hall with doors leading to classrooms, just as it was seven years ago. Now, however, it was silent. For a second I saw girls running, laughing, talking. I saw teachers. I heard the sounds of feet and the bell ringing. I felt the school was full of life. The silence screamed at me, though, a silence so terrible that it hurt my ears. I stood there alone. "My God, am I the only one who survived?" I cried. As I later found out, I was the only survivor from my kindergarten class. I couldn't cry anymore. I was too filled with pain. I felt terribly guilty for being alive, and that feeling was followed by terrible anger. I walked out of the school and never returned.

As I walked back to our building, I was approached by a middle-aged couple. They didn't say a word but just looked and looked at me. Timidly, the man spoke. "By any chance, is your name Basha?" he asked.

"No," I replied. "My name is Hanna."

The man put his arm around the woman as she began to cry. He looked at me through dreadfully sad eyes. "You look like we think our daughter might look," he said to me, "if she is alive." I felt very bad for them.

When I returned to our building, Mother had not moved. She was still sitting lifelessly on the sofa. I sat by her, hoping Father would come back soon.

When he returned, I could tell by his face that he had good news. He had gone to the Jewish community center where survivors could register. In this way, searching for family members was facilitated. He had found some people he knew there, unfortunately not many, and he, like every new arrival, was greeted with joy by those already there. Every life saved was a miracle. There he met survivors of concentration camps and learned from them the horrors of the inhumanity suffered by those in the camps. There was a long list of annihilated people, and it was growing rapidly with names of friends and relatives, old and young.

As he read the survivor list, he found a familiar name, Sznycer. This was my friend Hania's name. With this news he came to us, and I was overcome with the hope that she might have survived. We decided that I would run to her home and try to find her. Father had found accommodations while he was at the center, and he and Mother were going to someone's home for the night. It was getting dark when I ran to Hania's home, and when I got there I took the stairs up two at a time. When I finally stood in front of her door, I took a deep breath and knocked. Hania's older sister, Bella, opened the door. For a second she stood staring at me, then she called her mother.

"I am Hanna, I am Hanna," I kept repeating.

"Hanna Davidson!" Bella said.

"You've changed so much," Mrs. Sznycer said as she grabbed me. Tears ran as we all hugged. I was afraid to ask about my friend Hania, and they were afraid to ask about my family. In those times this was a very difficult question, and there was great fear in learning the answer. I didn't see Hania, and I didn't dare ask. Then her mother told me that Hania and her younger sister, Edzia, were attending evening classes to complete their interrupted education, but that they'd be home soon. We sat down and began telling each other our stories.

When Hania entered the room where we sat, I stood up without a word. Changed as we were, girls no longer, we still recognized each other instantly. Neither of us could speak. We were choking with tears. It was a very emotional time for everyone, and we were thankful for finding each other. I told them I was with my parents, which brought new tears, but we didn't know about Kazik and Marie and the rest of our family. I learned that their only son, Hania's brother, was killed in a concentration camp.

Later, when the evening meal was served, for the first time in many years I sat in a dining room around a table set with individual plates, forks, knives, and spoons. I'd almost forgotten what it was like to eat from one's own plate. After the meal, Hania's mother quietly asked me if I'd like to take a bath. I'd forgotten how dirty I was and how shabby my clothes were. Without hesitation I accepted her offer. Hania started to fill the bathtub with hot water—a bath all for me, alone! This was a luxury I couldn't remember. I felt dizzy and unreal, in a cloud of being and yet not being at the same time. With embarrassment I told Hania that I was covered with lice. Her mother provided some disinfectant, which I used happily. She told me she understood perfectly, because when they were liberated from the concentration camp and returned home after so many years, they went through the same thing.

I undressed in the bathroom and stepped into the heavenly warm water, letting it embrace me like a soft blanket. I washed my hair over and over again and scrubbed my skin until it turned red. I submerged in the wonderful water and let it cover me completely. I stayed in the tub for a long time, so long that Hania finally came in to see if I was all right. Then I dried myself with a clean towel and put on some clothes that Hania's mother gave me.

I stepped out of that bathroom a different person, clean and refreshed. We talked long into the night. When we finally went to bed, I slept, for the first time in many years, in a real bed with clean linen and rested my head on a soft pillow. Hania and I whispered and talked still, but not once did we touch on the subject of how we had survived.

The next day, after breakfast, we talked more. It was then that I learned what happened to some of my little friends. Hania didn't know how Runia, Annet, or Ruth died. It was presumed that they were taken to concentration camps and perished in gas chambers. Stefcia was forced, along with many other children, onto an old boat, which was then taken and sunk in the Baltic Sea. Iza, my foster sister, begged for bread on the streets of the ghetto until she froze to death. Teachers and other friends perished in different concentration camps or in gas chambers.

At midday Father knocked on the door and stood before us with a radiant and smiling face. "Marie and everyone in her family is alive!" he said. The commotion that followed this news need not be described, but this time the tears were happy ones.

Mother waited downstairs, and Father and I hurried to meet her. Then the three of us ran in the street, saying to each other, "Hurry, hurry." We reached Piotrkowska Street and continued running until we stopped in front of number 226. So familiar was this building with the same windows and entrance, so full of life. The porter opened the door and, recognizing us, let us in. We ran to Marie's door and rang the bell.

The door opened and there stood Nastusia, who had been our housekeeper before Jasia. "I prayed and prayed for this moment," she said, as tears filled her eyes. We all stood there with no strength left for one more step or one more word.

Marie approached the door. When she saw us she stopped, incapable of moving. We were all paralyzed with emotion. Finally, she whispered my parents' diminutive names, "Zochna, Ziamka." She looked at me and whispered, "Ala?," referring to Mother's younger sister.

I shook my head. "It's me, Hanna," I said.

"You're so grown up," she cried.

This was the joy we'd hoped and prayed for. We hugged, kissed, cried, and laughed, all at the same time.

Later, when Stephany came home, in order to avoid the shock of surprise, Marie slowly told her about our survival. We walked into the room as she sat on the sofa and surrounded her. Words were not necessary. Tears and hugs spoke for us. When Frank and his mother came home from work, there was more of the same.

The twins, Sylvia and Anne, came home from school, and we were surprised to find that they were big girls now. Vala, the Polish woman who had risked her life many times in order to save the lives of Frank, Marie, Stephany, and the twins, arrived. We had found our family! It was then that life returned to my mother's eyes.

Not everyone was there, however. We didn't know what had happened to Kazik. Frank's father and Henryk both died in concentration camps. Ala, Mother's sister, had a terrible death which was never revealed to Stephany or Mother. She and Grandmother Helen were coming through a nearby forest with wood and Ala was grabbed and raped by an SS man. Grandmother died after witnessing this attack. The SS man took Ala away with him, and when he tired of her, he sent her to a concentration camp. By this time she had lost her mind. She died in a gas chamber.

We talked throughout the night and exchanged stories of our survival. It is not possible to put into words the emotions we felt. We rejoiced in finding each other, and we cried for our lost family and friends. There were thirteen of us together in this crowded but happy home, thirteen of us who survived. We talked about Kazik and determined that in the morning we would start an investigation about him at the army headquarters. After many frustrating attempts, we were able to gather some news about a week later.

Frank was the one who came home with the wonderful news that Kazik was alive. He was an officer in the Polish army, stationed in a garrison in the mountains of southern Poland. Frank obtained permission to use a government car and, on his first day off, he drove south to find Kazik. He returned triumphant. Kazik was alive, and he was well. Immediately Father started the difficult task of requesting that Kazik be relieved from his military duties. In the end, Kazik was dismissed with honor and was awarded a medal for bravery in battle. When he finally came home, our reunion was indeed complete.

Then he told us what had happened to him. After the PPC was formed, the First Polish Division was organized. Kazik was drafted. Due to his academic standing he was placed in the ranks of combat engineers and dispatched to Ryazan so quickly that he wasn't able to let us know.

All superior officers were Russian, and most had very little or no knowledge of the Polish language. Since Kazik spoke both languages, he was considered to be very valuable. He was given the task of organizing a heavy artillery unit. The Polish army was in terrible condition. They were underfed, poorly clothed, and covered with lice. In July of 1944 they reached Praga, a suburb of Warsaw. At precisely that time, the underground army in Warsaw began a heroic uprising, fighting Nazi tanks and artillery with terribly insufficient weapons. The Polish army was eager to advance and help these partisans. But to their horror and terrible sorrow, the Soviet government forbade them to take any action because this would be against Stalin's plan. For three weeks Kazik witnessed the siege and the burning of Warsaw, which was completely destroyed.

In the middle of January a major offensive was launched and Warsaw was liberated. This offensive continued west, and Kazik was among the first to enter Berlin. Later, when he was on leave, he returned to Łódź. He went to our home, but we weren't there. The occupant would not let him in. He passed by Frank and Marie's home and saw lights in the window but didn't dare to inquire who lived there. He had no hope of finding any of his family alive.

12
MAKING A LIFE

We were all together again. I enrolled in the university for mathematics courses. Hania and I gathered young survivors, and we formed a wonderful small group. It was at this time that we found Lilly and Maryla, a classmate. Kazik and Vala were part of our group, and so was his friend, Romek. Kazik and Romek were the only two survivors of their entire unit. Gradually other solitary survivors joined us.

We learned that Frank, Marie, and all their family survived on false documents called "Aryan papers," which stated that they were Polish and Catholic. They hid in a small Polish town, Olsztyn, which is near Częstohowa, under Vala's supervision and direction. She risked her life for them, many times. To this day we admire, cherish, and love her dearly. In addition, in the attic of their little house they hid two other Jewish men. All of them survived, thanks to Vala.

Poland was now under Communist control. Before long, the UB, which was the Polish equivalent of the Soviet KGB, began arresting many people. Father, with his Bund affiliation, was in danger. It was clear to us that we would not escape the Communist regime in Soviet-dominated Poland and that we might not be able to continue living in Poland. With great sorrow we realized we were unwelcome in the land of our ancestors.

The situation worsened with the occasional outbreaks of pogroms. One of the worst ones was in Kielce, not too far from Łódź. It ended in the massacre of forty-one Jews. One of those killed was Lilly's brother-in-law. He died on the same day of his son's bris celebration. This traditional circumcision ceremony must be performed on every Jewish boy child's eighth day of life. During this joyful celebration, Lilly's sister was forced to mourn the loss of her husband. It

The Morgens family in Olsztyn (c. 1943). Back row (left to right): Marie's mother-in-law, Dobrysz Morgens, Marie, Stephanie, and Ala. Front row: Marie's twin daughters, Anne (left) and Sylvia (right).

was these pogroms which prompted us to make the painful decision to leave Poland.

Since being reunited with Marie and her family we had lived in their apartment—the four of us, Frank, Marie, Anna, Sylvia, Stephany, Frank's mother, his sister-in-law and her daughter Rita, and Vala. Now, sitting around the dining room table, we had long discussions on how to execute our exodus from Poland. Some of our friends decided to go to Palestine, but our family was inclined to go to the United States.

We began planning our emigration. Frank's brother, Joe, was an American citizen and he was working to obtain visas for his mother, Frank, Marie, Anna, and Sylvia. Marie's mother, Stephany, who was not a blood relative of Joe's, couldn't get one. Frank desperately looked for channels that would permit Stephany to leave Poland illegally, the only possibly way for her to leave. He went to the port city of Gdynia, where he found a Swedish boat, the *Pele*. He begged the captain to take Stephany, but without legal documents this was impossible and his plea was not accepted. However, Frank met a cook

Fifty years later, a memorial program was held at 7 Plenty Street, the site of the infamous Kielce pogrom of July 1946. Photograph by Steve Lipman. From *Jewish Week*, June 28, 1996. Reprinted with permission.

on the freighter and, taking a chance, he offered a bribe to the cook and asked him to take Stephany aboard the ship. The bribe was accepted—Stephany would go as a stowaway.

My parents, Kazik, and I were denied permission to enter the United States, despite enormous efforts put forth by my Uncle George. The reason given was: we had survived by living in Russia. We were deemed undesirable elements who had been exposed to the Communist regime, and as such, we were not acceptable. There was no other choice but to pursue illegal emigration.

It was time for me to make a very difficult decision. Most of my friends were Zionists, ready to fight, which they did in the years to come, with courage and heroism until the Jewish state was born. One friend, in particular, asked me to go to Palestine with him. Father, as a Bundist, believed in the possibility of rebuilding the Jewish community in any country. This meant that I had to choose between going to Palestine with my friend or staying with my parents. Hardship, danger, and the long, difficult road did not scare me. What frightened me was the separation from my entire family with the possibility of not seeing them again. Crying, I went to Mother hoping that she would give me a magic solution.

"What shall I do?" I asked.

"Only you know the answer, and only you know your feelings and your heart," Mother responded. "The decision has to be yours. Whatever you do, we will support your decision and will always love you." Sobbing, I threw myself in her arms. She hugged me and tenderly stroked my head. In that instant, I realized that I could not leave my parents at this point in my life.

We cherished every minute that was left to us with the whole family. Vala, so devoted to our family and so dear to us, refused to stay in Poland. Since she couldn't go with Frank and Marie, she decided to join us. Dora Mess was the sixth person in our group. Dora was an acquaintance of ours from before the war. Father met her on the street one day, and a well-known scene repeated itself—stunned silence, tears of emotion, questions, questions, questions, and finally, the story of the last seven years.

Dora was a divorcée. Her daughter married shortly before the war and moved to Piotrkow with her husband. They entered the ghetto there, and there they perished. Dora, who had been a French

Mrs. Mess, Israel, 1954.

teacher, remained on the Aryan side of Warsaw, where she worked as a governess for a Polish family's young child. The family she worked for was strongly anti-Semitic, and she had to listen to expressions of outright hatred toward the Jews, and even to agreement with German actions when the Warsaw ghetto's annihilation was in progress. All the while her heart was bleeding for her child and her people.

After the war her employers moved to Łódź and, not knowing what to do, she kept her position. When Father brought her to us, she was able to let go of her pretense and become herself once again. Sobbing, she implored us to help her out of the trap she was in. "Take me into your family," she begged. "I have no one. No place to be, no place to go." Thus, Dora Mess became one of us.

This emotional scene was a familiar one. It was one more experience of postwar confusion during the moving of masses of humanity.

Jewish organizations provided help for refugees crossing the Polish-German border. We were notified that one group of Jews would leave in two days and were promised six train tickets. We were told to be ready for departure on Saturday evening. While it didn't take us long to put our meager belongings in bags, it was very difficult to say goodbye. Each of us was heading in a different direction, not knowing where, just to escape.

We sat for our last family meal in Łódź. Feelings of immensely important and drastic changes in our lives were reflected on our faces and in our moods. With sadness and tenderness we reminisced about the past. With fear and uncertainty we contemplated our future. Tears shamelessly streamed from our eyes, wetting each other's cheeks. The last hug, the last kiss, and the last goodbyes. According to an old superstition, to ensure a safe trip and a reunion with loved ones we sat in silence for a few seconds before leaving the house. I closed my eyes, engraving the moment in my mind. Then we picked up our belongings, and the six of us walked out.

Stephany left for Gdynia the next day. The cook of the Swedish ship hid her in his cabin. Once in Sweden, she was arrested for entering the country illegally. She was released only after her brother-in-law, Professor Herman Muntz, a long time resident of Stockholm, took her into his custody.

Frank, Marie, and their family left Poland a few days later on their way to Sweden.

13
OUT OF POLAND

At the train station we joined other Jewish refugees. We were divided into small groups according to political associations within the Zionist Party. The one assigned to us was Revisionist, because Father's friend was a member of it, and he obtained our place for the duration of our traveling. We boarded the train, and before long the whistle announced our departure. As the train gained speed, taking us farther and farther from home, I remember the last sight of Łódź as the city lights disappeared in the distance. Those lights are still there, in my mind, for I never saw Łódź again.

The next morning we reached Wałbrzych, a German city on the Czechoslovakian border. Although the city became Polish after the war, it retained its German character and German population. The streets were clean and quiet, lined with neat little houses. Well-fed German children played in front of the houses. I couldn't restrain my resentment of these children because I knew that their fathers, grandfathers, and uncles had starved, tortured, and killed innocent Jewish children who were just like them. We stayed in Wałbrzych for two days awaiting permission to continue our journey. At the end of the second day our group leader announced that we should be ready to move the following morning.

"We are ready," was the unanimous response of our seventy voices. It was a short trip to Frydlant [v Čechách, Czechoslovakia], a very small frontier town between Poland and Czechoslovakia. It was a mile and a half from the station to the border customs house. It was unseasonably hot for fall, and we worried that the long walk would be too much for Mother and Mrs. Mess if they had to carry any luggage. Finding transportation in this remote area was not possible. As we wondered what to do, a horse cart appeared in the distance. As it came closer we waved to the old man who was walking beside the cart. Surprised, he stopped the cart.

"Would you take us to the border?" asked Father.

The man scratched his head. "It's opposite to the direction that I am going," he responded.

"I have two hundred zlotys," Father said as he pulled the money out of his pocket. The temptation was too big. The man turned the cart around and we loaded it with our luggage. Mother and Mrs. Mess sat in the cart, but the rest of us walked.

We finally saw a building with about five hundred refugees gathered, either sitting on the grass or walking back and forth in the hot sun. There was no place in shade for us to rest and stretch our tired feet.

"Here, come here," Vala screamed to us. "I found a place under a tree!" We ran to the treasured spot and sat down to rest. Vala walked away from us. In a few minutes she returned with bread, butter, sausages, and even some apples from a nearby store. What a feast! We ate in that shade, watching cart after cart loaded with bundles and suitcases pass by going toward the frontier. We hoped that soon our turn would come.

As the sky reddened by the rays of the setting sun, cool breezes blew between the leaves of our tree, bringing relief from the heat. It was time to seek shelter for the night. Unwillingly I picked up my bundle and got up from this pleasant place to follow the rest of my family into a building which provided accommodations for all the refugees. It was dirty and smelled very bad. We entered a large, overcrowded room with small windows that didn't provide much light. There were no beds, so the only place to sleep was on the filthy floor. Vala found a broom and we swept an area in the corner, put down cleaner boards we had found outside, and settled in for the night. News of border crossings filled our ears. The search is very strict, someone said. Another person said refugees are coming back, unable to cross the border. The tension in that room was unbelievable. Everyone was concerned. One small red-headed man next to us was extremely nervous and constantly repacked his suitcase. I noticed that he had five rings on his fingers, which was very unusual. No wonder he was so upset. We were concerned that his unlawful possessions might affect all of us.

"Do not listen to gossip," Father said. "We have nothing to be concerned about. Let's get some rest. Sleep."

I followed his advice, put my head on my elbow, and fell asleep in spite of the hard floor, the constant noise, and the shuffle of feet. I opened my eyes just as the morning sun was peeking through a small dirty window.

Every day we would ask the same question: "When will we be able to cross the border?" But nobody knew. So we waited. And waited.

Four days later a bit of information reached us. If yesterday's party was able to get across, our turn would be tomorrow, at noon. At twelve o'clock the following day we were ready to leave. Luck was with us this time, and we got orders to move on. Our luggage was loaded in carts which would be taken to the frontier along with three people as representatives from our party, which now consisted of four hundred people. We all had to walk a distance of two miles to the custom point. Four long columns of women, children, and men, young and old, began the slow walk on the dusty road. By three we reached the point of division between two countries. On one side a plain stake bore a sign: *Poland*. Fifty meters from it stood another identical pole but with the inscription: *Czechoslovakia*. We were told to sit down and wait outside the customs house. It was a peaceful country afternoon, and we enjoyed hearing birds sing their tunes. As the sun dipped the blue sky began to darken, turning orange, then red. The beauty of the sunset was disturbed by a gray cloud on the horizon. A storm was approaching. Lightning illuminated the dark sky in the distance just as the customs searches began. It was a very slow process, and when our time came in the middle of the night it was raining. The wind blew harder and harder. We grabbed our belongings and ran to the customs house. When we reached there, we were soaking wet and cold. Our turn came at one in the morning. At this time we were standing in line shivering in our wet clothing. The whole search ended in one question: "Do you have any cigarettes?" We did not.

We entered a dark room so crowded that we could hardly sit down with our legs crossed, and this is how we passed the rest of the night. In the morning, we waited for further instructions. Time passed slowly, especially so because everyone was anxious to cross the border. At last, two customs officers came and told us to form four lines, and we began to move forward. The customs barrier was opened and we left Polish soil, crossing no man's land to the Czechoslovakian barrier. My heart was beating so fast I could hardly breathe, and my legs felt weak. I turned to look at Poland—for the last time. Then Czechoslovakian officers opened their barrier and we crossed the frontier, walking with our belongings, and entered another customs house for another search. This search was very detailed, but here only cigarettes were confiscated. It was an exceptionally easy border crossing, arranged by our organization, which used large bribes to smoothe the way, and was facilitated by Poland's eagerness to get rid of Jews and the Czechs' willingness to accept bribes.

A tractor pulling three platforms was before us, and we quickly threw our belongings on one and jumped aboard. Immediately the motor roared and the tractor advanced, pulling us to a temporary camp fifteen kilometers from the frontier. We were all quiet as we entered the camp, and uneasy. Although barbed wire had been removed, the camp had obviously been used as a concentration camp by the Germans. Rows of barracks stood on both sides of a grass-covered road. Each building consisted of a dark room with bunk beds and straw mattresses. We were given blankets and pillows and a simple meal with plenty of bread and coffee. I did not sleep that night. As I lay on my bunk, thoughts of the previous occupants of the same plank bed tormented me. I could feel their presence—the air was thick with their spirits.

We stayed in this camp for two days. We were told we'd be crossing the border between Czechoslovakia and Austria as Czech workers and were advised to destroy any nonessential documents written in Polish and to conceal those of importance. I remember sitting around the only table in the barracks, painfully examining each of our papers and few photographs with inscriptions in Polish. We used scissors to cut the words from the photos, leaving only the figures and faces of those who were not with us anymore. We were also warned not to speak Polish or Yiddish in the presence of strangers and not to engage in any conversations with them.

The crossing itself was, in fact, as easy as the previous one. We all knew we were safe at last as we left behind the Communist countries and entered a part of Europe, Allied countries, which were friendly to us. We breathed the sweet air of freedom, inhaling it with all the capacity of our lungs.

We were informed that we would proceed to Vienna, and I was delighted to be able to see this famous city. At our arrival in Vienna we were directed to a displaced persons (DP) camp, which, as all other camps were, was sponsored by UNRRA (United Nations Relief and Rehabilitation Administration), an organization that provided shelters, food, and help for refugees from Communist countries moving across Europe to numerous destinations. In addition, we were helped by JOINT, the American Jewish Joint Distribution Committee (officially AJJDC, but more commonly referred to as JOINT), an American Jewish organization. Our hospitality house was a huge facility previously occupied by the Rothschild Hospital. Our family was moved to a large building with a beautiful facade and huge, heavy wooden doors that opened to a reception hall exiting in a courtyard enclosed by buildings which had been used for the hospital. Each floor had rooms or halls for patients and medical staff. Now these rooms were assigned to us. We shared one of the rooms with many others. Our family, Vala, and Mrs. Mess stayed together, occupying one corner of the room. At the entrance hall were long tables with receptionists and piles of forms. We formed registration lines and each of us had to fill in a form. I remember mine: last name, first name, place and date of birth. There was no question asking my address—I had none. My home was now whatever camp I was in, DP camps. I asked a woman at the table, "What is a DP camp?"

"This is a displaced persons camp," she replied. I understood then that we were no longer refugees but rather we were homeless. We were not citizens of any country, and no country was willing to accept us at this time. This reality hit me very hard. I felt suspended, not knowing where I would be tomorrow and completely dependent on the help of strangers for my existence. While I fully appreciated their willingness to help, after so many years of struggling to survive it was not easy to accept the idea that our struggle would still continue.

Just as we settled down, a commotion outside disturbed us and two Jewish policemen walked into our room. Somehow the story spread around camp that our family was trying to smuggle a Polish Gentile woman out of Poland. Since it was known that Nazi collaborators during the occupation now pretended to be Jewish refugees to

Registration card issue to Hanna by the Jewish Workers Committee in Łódź, 1946.

escape punishment for war crimes, it was understandable why the Jewish authorities came to investigate who this person was.

They came to us, identified Vala, and escorted her to the main office, taking Father with them. I loudly protested and must have raised my voice. As a result, I was told to follow Vala and Father. From a main office Vala was ushered into a separate room to our left, and a door closed behind her. We were escorted to the larger room and approached a heavy table at the back of the room where some men were seated. Two chairs were placed in the center of this area and we were told to sit, facing these men. Father was very nervous as the Jewish camp police began to ask questions. "Your name, and the reason you are here, please," they asked Father. He answered. Then I was asked the same question.

"You know my name," I replied angrily. "And the reason is obvious why I am here." My tone of voice and my abrupt manner were not received kindly.

"What is kosher?" they asked me.

"Kosher is Jewish dietary laws," I answered.

"How is kosher meat prepared?" was the next question. "Every Jewish girl knows that."

I know now, but I didn't know then. "Do you think this was allowed to be taught in the U.S.S.R.?" I angrily responded. "We survived the war in any way we could only to find ourselves under arrest by Jews? Furthermore, Vala, also arrested here, endangered her life many, many times to save members of my family and two other Jews as well." The more I rebelled, the more hostility we were shown from these prosecutors. We were informed that we'd be deported back to Poland. Father turned white and desperately tried to explain the situation.

Vala was being interrogated at the same time. Her story was the same as ours. When asked about the men she'd hidden in the attic, she gave their names, one being Sasha Winnikow. Upon hearing Sasha's name, one of the interrogators became very excited. "Sasha is alive? You saved him? He is my best friend and I have not been able to find him."

A commotion outside stopped the questioning. The commotion was caused by Mother. When we were detained, Mother, Kazik, and Mrs. Mess went to the courtyard looking for help, trying to find somebody who could identify us. Suddenly, from a second-story window came a shout: "Mrs. Davidson! You're here! Do you recognize me?" Seconds later a woman was in the courtyard running to Mother, crying and hugging her. "You survived," she said through her sobs.

Mother recognized the daughter of her dear friend, a girl who had been her student in Łódź. She had lost most of her family and, like us, was seeking a new life by escaping from Poland. This unexpected encounter was most welcome at this difficult moment. Mother told her what was happening. Together they came to the room where we were being held. Father turned his head, surprised to see Mother accompanied by a familiar face. With tears in his eyes he took her in his arms. "Thank God you survived!" he whispered to her.

Just at that time another refugee came in. His name was Zev Sztajnert. He had heard about the Gentile woman being held, and he came to tell his story. "I know about this woman," he said. "She was in Olsztyn, and I was there, too. I was sent to work at Hasag, a slave labor plant near Olsztyn," he said. "It was in Olsztyn that this woman and the Morgens family were hiding. From time to time some of us were sent to Olsztyn to work, and once I saw this woman. I overheard a shopkeeper whisper, 'Here comes the woman who hides the Jews.' I admire her greatly," Zev told the Jewish police.

Vala was cleared, released, and became an instant hero. I was reprimanded for my behavior, but peace was restored to the camp. Now everyone wanted to shake hands with Vala and everyone was extra nice to her. She even was given a double ration of food. That evening Zev came to see Vala. Through the window of our room I saw them walking around the courtyard, talking and laughing.

The next day we ventured into the city. We walked only a few blocks when to our horror we saw an approaching army unit in familiar sand-gray uniforms. It was a Soviet army detachment singing Russian songs as they marched. In panic, we ran back to the shelter, afraid that we had fallen under Soviet rule. It was explained to us that at the present time Vienna was divided into three zones: the Soviet, American, and French. It happened that the Rothschild Hospital was located in the Soviet zone but under U.S. control. This knowledge calmed us, and we resumed our journey into the city.

I had imagined Vienna as a sunny, happy city full of music and life. But this is not what we saw. The splendid buildings, parks with monuments, and streets lined with trees, museums, opera houses, theaters, gardens and the Danube River were still there. But many of the famous buildings were heavily damaged and burned. Scars of the war left the city sad and lifeless.

We stayed in Vienna three days. A new transport filled with refugees was on the way, and our space was needed to accommodate them. We were to be relocated to the next camp. With this move, we lost our hope to start steps toward emigration to America from Vienna.

This was the beginning of our wandering from one camp to another, camps which had such a short time ago witnessed inhuman crimes still so alive in all our minds. More than five hundred camps were spread throughout Europe like deadly webs. How was it possible that the existence of so many camps was unknown, as claimed?

14
CAMP ON THE DANUBE

From Vienna we traveled to Linz, an industrial city on the Danube River, little damaged by the war. The train didn't stop at the station, however, but continued until we were out of the city limits. The train slowed and came to a complete stop at a camp located on both sides of the railway. This camp, like the one before, had been used by the Nazis as a concentration camp. Entering such camps was always shocking for us.

As we unloaded our belongings we were greeted by earlier arrivals who searched for loved ones who might be alive. We did not meet anyone we knew. To the right of the entrance were rows of wooden barracks, and to the left was a grassy square with tables covered with white sheets and medical supplies. Behind the tables stood nurses and camp officials. Single lines were formed, and one by one we approached them for registration.

"Go to the next line for vaccination," we were ordered. "Roll your sleeves up, please." The nurse had syringes ready and quickly I got a shot in my arm and stepped forward. The person behind me took my place.

"Bend your head now, please." I did what I was told and my hair was sprayed with DDT. "Unbutton your blouse, please." My face turned red, but I obeyed. I felt a stream of cold powder on my breasts and stomach. "Turn around." The powder ran down my back, reaching my legs.

This was not the first nor the last time we would undergo this procedure. There was great need to prevent the spread of epidemics among the multitudes of refugees. I was thankful for the help but wish some personal sensitivity had been taken into consideration.

After this process we collected cots, blankets, and utensils and were directed to our barracks. A wooden door led to a long room where several families and a few single persons were settling in for the night. Our group of six stayed together, putting our cots in a row, one next to the other. We made our beds and put our belongings underneath them. When this was done it was time for the evening meal. Taking our tin plates and cups, we walked to the mess hall. Coffee with bread and butter was already on the tables, and we had as much of this as we wanted.

It was twilight when we walked back a narrow dirt path to our barracks. Walking on this path, I felt my feet burning as I visualized the footprints of so many who had walked here before me. Big feet and small ones, feet barely learning to walk on their own, barefooted or with toes sticking out of worn-out shoes, feet with blisters or frostbite, feet on their last journey. I ran to the barracks and threw myself on the cot. All night long I had nightmares hearing footsteps around me. Finally darkness began to disappear, silencing the sound of the feet.

Our stay in Linz came to an end after a few days, and as always we were asked to return all that was given to us during our stay in this camp. We folded the cots, rolled the blankets and the pillows, gathered spoons, forks, cups, and plates, and returned them. Then our group marched in double lines to the train and boarded a boxcar. Destination unknown.

15
WEGSHEID, AUSTRIA

Many hours later the train stopped at a station in Wegsheid, Austria. I jumped off the boxcar, glad to be on solid ground. It felt good to stretch my legs during the walk to the next camp. Once again all the formalities were repeated, including disinfection. I must admit, thanks to the strict hygiene standards, there were no outbreaks of contagious disease in any of our camps, despite the great numbers of people passing through.

These barracks looked a little better than in the other camps and indeed the accommodations proved to be better. To our delight we six got a room to ourselves. Ours was a small room, the first one on the right as we entered the hall. Opposite the door was a tiny window under which was a table with two chairs. We put cots for Mrs. Mess, Vala, and myself against the wall to the right of the window. Kazik put his on the left, and my parents placed theirs in the corner behind the door. Everything was primitive and simple, but at last we were alone in a room, and it was wonderful. There was a single nail on the wall and we were able to hang our coats. On the table we neatly stacked six tin cups, plates, spoons, and forks. I remember lying down on my freshly made cot, luxuriating in not being in the constant presence of strangers.

The barracks stood around a big square covered with grass. In the far corner was a kitchen, mess hall, and the office. From our room I could see the busy square filled with people coming and going in all directions. This square was the center of all activities from early in the morning until late in the evening. We decided that one of us would go to the kitchen with containers to bring coffee, bread, and butter, and we ate in our room. At noon, in the dining room, we had canned soup, meat and vegetables, and at supper we had coffee, milk, sugar, and bread. All supplies were military rations left for the use of the camp. There was a general hope that we would stay in this place. Winter was almost upon us, it was getting cold, and we were eager to begin processes toward our emigration to America.

We looked for work. Father, after meeting some friends, obtained work in the main office. Kazik found a job in the mechanical department. I was accepted as a helper in administration. We were paid a few cigarettes a day for our work. It was wonderful! Mrs. Mess came to life and enthusiastically formed a group of people interested in learning English. We all were eager to participate, except for Mother and Vala. Mother's apathy did not surprise us, but the change in Vala did.

From the first day of our arrival at this camp, Vala would frequently disappear. Father, as head of the family, felt responsible for Vala's welfare and asked for an explanation of her frequent disappearances. She never gave him a straight answer. "I am having a very good time," was her only response. Later we learned that there was a group of young Zionists among the refugees and that this group was involved in military training sponsored by the Hagana. The Hagana was formed in Palestine under direction of British Officer Orde Wingate, who trained small military units in *kibbutzim* (collective farms). These units became the nucleus of the future Israeli army. Some members of the Hagana were sent to Jewish communities, especially in Europe, to recruit young people. One of them arrived in our camp, organizing volunteers to be trained as fighters. After a day of intensive training the group would gather around bonfires in the evening, singing Hebrew songs and dancing the hora, a traditional Jewish dance. Vala was greatly attracted to their activities, and to Zev Sztajnert, who was among them.

Then one day Vala came to Father. "I am in love with Zev," she said.

"I have to find out what kind of person he is," Father told her. He approached Mr. Frydman, our camp leader, who knew everybody.

"Zev is absolutely honest, hard-working, and a good person," Mr. Frydman said. "I trust him completely." Others who knew Zev gave this same opinion to Father.

"I would like to talk to him," Father told Vala. "He can come at any time."

Zev came a few days later. "I never forgot Vala," he began, "not from the first time I saw her in Olsztyn. It was destiny that we met again. I am thirty-one years old and fully understand my obligations. I love Vala. I ask for Vala's hand. I promise to take care of her, support her, cherish her. I couldn't find a better wife than Vala."

"I want Vala to be happy," Father responded. "Her qualities are beyond any words. She is an exceptional human being." He emphasized their different backgrounds and religions and the difficulties of their union. Both Zev and Vala felt they belonged together, however, and stated that they were ready to overcome any future hardships. And so Father gave them his blessing.

In the middle of these exciting events, our transfer to another camp was announced. This was a hard blow to me because we would go in different directions. All refugees hoping to emigrate to the United States had to go to the American zone in Germany as DPs. Those who dreamed of Palestine as their future home would travel to Italy. This meant that Vala would marry Zev immediately. The little ceremony took place the following evening. We all helped Vala to dress. I picked wildflowers, which were growing behind the barracks, and made a beautiful bouquet. Vala looked so happy and radiant. Wedding vows were exchanged in front of two witnesses because there was no judge. According to Jewish law, this is acceptable in such cases. The ceremony consisted of a solemn promise, a breaking of glass, and a kiss. Then Zev and Vala were pronounced husband and wife. A small reception followed in the mess hall. Food was provided by the camp, even some wine for a toast, and cake. We had singing and dancing to celebrate this unusual union, this marriage of a Gentile woman to a Zionist, as well as their decision to make a life in Palestine.

After the festivities ended it was time to go to our room. It hit me then that Vala would be gone from us forever. I ran to Zev and pleaded with him to allow Vala to spend this last night with us. We stayed up all night talking, laughing, and crying. When the sun rose, it was time to prepare for our departure. We were asked to return camp utensils and to be ready to leave early in the afternoon. Zev and Vala helped us drag our belongings to the train, where we found the number of our boxcar. They helped us load our things, we had time for a brief goodbye, and then we embarked on the train. From the open door I waved to Vala and Zev, forcing a smile. I did not want them to see me cry.

Zev and Vala left the next day. From this point on, Zionist groups were on their own. While they were sponsored by the Hagana, they had to cross the Alps illegally in order to reach Italy on their dangerous voyage to Palestine.

16
A MILITARY COMPOUND

We left Austria and entered Germany, moving deeper into the American zone. The next morning, when the train finally stopped, we found ourselves inside a military compound left by the American army. It was spread throughout a huge field; hundreds of tents stood in rows divided by neat grassy strips. At the end of the camp were outside facilities and showers. In the middle of one side were modern barracks. One was used as a clinic and office. Another was a kitchen and food storage area.

Registration was very quick. Our documents were stamped with our day of arrival and signed by an official. Next we entered the clinic. When I saw the white table with trays, syringes, and DDT, I began to shake. The prospect of another vaccination and another spraying with DDT was just too much. When my turn came, the nurse, with a syringe in her hand, told me to roll up my sleeve; I could not. I stood motionless. "We were sprayed and vaccinated just a short time ago," I finally was able to say. "This will be the fourth time for me."

"Sorry. This is obligatory for all new arrivals," the nurse responded.

"I will not have it!" I cried.

"Step aside then," she said to me. "You cannot enter this camp."

I got out of line, tears running down my face, and moved to the side. Mother and Mrs. Mess came to me, trying to calm me. "Remember how we were covered with lice?" Mother said. "Did you already forget the miserable itching and fear of sickness? We don't want this to happen again. The unpleasant moments are worth the security of our health and the prevention of epidemics. With thousands of refugees here, that can happen. Hanna, being here is the only chance for us."

I knew my outburst of anger was out of place, but I could not help it. Resigned, I entered the line. I was sprayed. I rolled up my sleeve and received a shot. The red marks of the previous vaccination were still visible.

When we finished, our line moved toward long tables out in the field. Huge pots were on the tables. Breakfast. Many people were gathered there. After collecting a tin plate, a cup, and silverware, we joined them. The food was distributed in amazing order. Soon we were eating bread, scrambled eggs which had been prepared from powdered eggs, and drinking coffee with milk. In addition, we were served a funny-looking brownish lump of something. We didn't know what it was. I tasted a tiny amount, but it stuck to my teeth. It felt grainy like dirt, but it tasted sweet. We called it "mud" and none of us liked to eat it. What strange food these Americans give us, we all commented. However, with the passing of time we got used to it, and many of us even grew to like it quite a bit, especially on bread with jelly. I still enjoy peanut butter this way.

At this camp we were assigned ten people to a military tent, which our family shared with five strangers. Dressing and undressing was very uncomfortable, but we mastered the art of doing this underneath a cover while still in bed. The days were long and monotonous. We had no newspapers, no books, no radios, no electricity. Only the moon provided light during the night. It was getting cold, and eating outside in the open was uncomfortable. We had plenty of food, but existence on the charity of others was demoralizing.

New transports arrived frequently, and we would greet them, always with the hope of finding someone we knew. One day as we watched new arrivals, a family who lived with us in Soviet Ukraine got off the train. Another time we found an old family friend from Łódź. The joy of finding someone known alive among thousands of strangers is indescribable.

During long hours in the evenings, we dreamed about our futures and imagined how our life would be in a new country. But each passing day diminished our hopes. The happiest person among us was Mrs. Mess, who, after so much suffering, was not alone anymore. Her gratitude had no limits.

Registration started for transport to another camp, possibly near the city of Frankfurt. We jumped at the opportunity to be closer to a

big city and registered. After a few days the train arrived. We returned the camp possessions, received food for the trip and the
number of our boxcar, and headed west.

17
BABENHAUSEN

I woke from an uncomfortable sleep with the first gray light of early morning, momentarily confused by the monotonous rocking. I quickly remembered we were in the train we'd boarded the previous day. One by one, people got up and began gathering their belongings. Tired, we were all anxious to reach our next destination.

Babenhausen was a beautiful small town of less than five thousand inhabitants which stood about twelve miles south of Frankfurt. The whole area was surrounded by forests of old trees impressive in their beauty and serenity. It was impossible to understand that in the middle of this breathtaking scenery was a place where the most horrific crimes were committed.

The train continued for a couple more miles before stopping at a small building with a wooden platform in front. Glad to reach our destination, we prepared to jump from the train. Suddenly we saw in front of us a camp surrounded with barbed wire and iron gates at the entrance. On top of the gate was an inscription: *Arbeit Macht Frei*, which means "Work Makes (one) Free," the ominous slogan over German death camp gates. At first there was deadly silence. Then loud voices called for resistance. Those who had jumped from the train turned back and reentered the boxcars. The nightmare of that sight weighed heavily on us all, especially on former inmates who had been liberated just a short time ago from camps such as this one. Many feared that we were betrayed.

"We can't trust anybody," passengers screamed, "not even the Americans. We will never pass those gates again!"

"We should trust the Americans," others hollered. "The Americans liberated the camps and wouldn't put us back in them!"

No one was willing to enter the barbed wire enclosure of the death camp. There was no UNRRA delegation at the station and nobody with whom we could talk. Unanimously the decision was made that we should attract the attention of the train staff. To accomplish this, we held a sit-in. In a few minutes everybody was in the boxcars—the station platform was deserted. We sat, facing the dreadful sight that stirred terrible wounds. We worked as one and collected all available food to distribute equally at meal time. We had a supply of bread and cans with meat for all of us, but most could not eat. As the day was ending, gray twilight embraced the earth, forming eerie shadows around the barbed wire and gates. I could almost see the ghosts of familiar faces looking at us through the wire. We sat inside the boxcar in total darkness throughout the sleepless night.

Somehow we were able to contact the UNRRA mission in Frankfurt and informed them of our dilemma. The next morning two young rabbis who were army chaplains came to find out what was wrong. When they saw the camp, they understood our refusal to enter this place, but they tried to calm us. "The American authorities understand," one of the rabbis told us, "but the influx of refugees is enormous. No one is prepared to take care of moving such masses of humanity across Europe, and therefore every available space and bed must be used." The other rabbi begged us to trust the American administration, which, he told us, had the best intentions. But all their arguments had no effect on the strikers, and we continued to sit. The rabbis left for Frankfurt.

That evening, the two rabbis returned and brought another rabbi with them. He was the head chaplain for the American army. He apologized for speaking to us in German, but he did not know Polish and we did not know English. He again emphasized the enormous task of moving such huge masses of people and asked for our understanding. "Winter is coming," he said, "and tents are not suitable for housing you in cold weather. I promise you, I give you my word of honor, this camp is not a concentration camp. The barbed wire can be removed immediately. Please vacate the train and let it return to Poland to bring more people who are waiting. If you cannot make yourselves do this, there will be no other choice. You will have to return with the train." He ended his speech with a blessing, wishing us new homes soon and an end to our homelessness. His commanding personality, gentleness, and logical arguments were impressive. Little by little we, the rebels, stepped down from the train and reluctantly entered the camp. The rabbis left, apologizing for the clumsiness of the American authorities. However, we fully understood that without the Americans we would still be in Poland, and we were thankful for their help.

As I entered the gates I closed my eyes at the moment I was under the arch and felt the anguish of the prisoners. Inside, enclosed by barbed wire, I stepped on soil permeated with blood and so much suffering. After a few days the barbed wire and the gates were removed, as we had been promised.

Except for our group and the assigned staff, the camp was completely empty. Rows of wooden and aluminum barracks stood in a big meadow surrounded by forests. The only clearing was at the gates and the platform for the train. The long barracks at the back of the camp served as a lavatory. It had taps with running cold water. In front was an office with many small rooms, and next to that was a clinic. The kitchen and mess hall were on the far right of the camp.

As soon as all required formalities ended we were directed to a wooden barracks. The door opened to a big room with a few small windows on the opposite long wall. Against this wall stood twenty parallel bunk beds and a small locker next to each one. A few single light bulbs hung from the low ceiling. We were lucky to get five beds in one of the corners. We made our beds, unpacked, and stored our belongings. Afterwards we went to the lavatory and washed, then went to the mess hall for an evening meal of coffee, bread, butter, and cheese.

Mother and Mrs. Mess were both at the point of exhaustion. We returned to our barracks quickly so they could go to bed and begin to recover their strength. After the drama of the past two days, all of us were weary and the camp was quiet.

In the morning, we began another adjustment to this new camp. Even though sharing a barracks among twenty people was not pleasant, we all hoped we would stay in this camp for the duration of winter. To create privacy, we constructed a little place where each of us could wash and dress undisturbed. We found pieces of wood with which we built a frame on one side of the door. The frame was covered with blankets which formed walls. One side was left loose and served as an entrance. Above this flap was placed a hook and a small hat. Whoever entered would remove the hat from the hook as a signal that the tiny room was occupied. Inside the cubicle we put a basin on a stand, a pitcher with water which each of us had to bring from the lavatory, and a chair. Surprisingly, we never had difficulty in taking turns to occupy this tiny spot of privacy. It was a blessing for each of us to have the luxury of seclusion.

The main events of the day were meals. Distribution of food three times a day was orderly and quick. All food was delivered from military supplies and consisted of coffee, rolls, and peanut butter for breakfast and soup, meat, and vegetables from cans for lunch and dinner. The meat I most remember is Spam, which I loved in the beginning. But after endless repetition, sometimes twice a day, it became abhorrent. Usually one of us would go to the mess hall and bring the family meal back to the barracks. We sat on two beds and pretended we were sitting around a table, the five of us, enjoying family meals.

Each day new transports would come and soon the camp was full. I met many new people and made new friends. Before long we formed a group of six: myself; my new girlfriend, who was in the camp with her mother; three lonely young men from different cities in Poland; and Kazik. How lucky we were, Kazik and I, to have our entire family!

Mrs. Mess organized English classes once again, mostly to keep us young people occupied. We studied in our barracks, sitting on beds as we worked. She took the lessons very seriously and made us study hard. The elders approved of any kind of education in any circumstances, and even those with no parents were pressed to learn. Young people were considered to be community responsibilities. After classes, our group stayed together. On rare occasions we caught a ride in a UNRRA truck and went into town. It was a distraction for us to just walk on the streets and window shop. We didn't have any money to spend, of course, and I remember that we all felt resentful of German teenagers who were living normal lives while we were suspended in the emptiness of camps.

The six of us developed close friendships. Inevitably, one of the boys and my girlfriend fell in love. I became the lone queen of our gang and enjoyed the courtship of the two other boys. We'd wander together around the camp or hike in the forest. With time, more young people joined our group.

At the far edge of the camp stood old abandoned tents in which prisoners had been held. In memory of them a rustic monument was built. With the help of the administration we cleared a small square of land, forming a little plaza. In the middle, on a grassy circle bordered with stones painted white, a simple gray concrete block with a white and blue dome was erected. On the front, black letters were framed with a black band, forming an inscription, which translates as follows: *Remembering six million of our brothers martyred at the hand of Nazis.* A small bench was placed to one side of the monument, underneath a tree, and we spent many afternoons there.

Mother and Mrs. Mess sought companionship, as old friends do, with those who had common memories. Mrs. Mess formed a special friendship with a young couple who had both lost their entire families. They married, escaped Poland, and hoped eventually to get to Palestine. They had a baby girl just a few months old. Mrs. Mess saw the young woman as the daughter she had lost and painfully pictured what might have been. The first time she held the young woman's baby, she hugged the little girl, rocking her gently, and sang a quiet lullaby. Choked with tears, she thought of the grandbaby she would never have. From that day on, they were inseparable.

In addition to all we'd been through, Mother was not doing well. For long years she'd been denied the opportunity to sculpt or paint. As an artist, this was devastating to her. Without her art she seemed lost and withdrawn. None of us knew how to help her.

Father was desperate for some kind of work and asked the head of the camp, who happened to be a French Jew, to take him as a voluntary worker. Father spoke some French and good German, and so his offer was accepted. He worked in the department of registration. "I regained my pride," he told us, "because I stopped being a freeloader." He became a staff member and as such obtained certain privileges. He was paid two bars of Hershey's chocolate and three packs of cigarettes a week. As soon as he established himself, he obtained work for Kazik and me as helpers in the office, and also for as many of the other young people as he could. We earned one chocolate bar a week. The chocolate we shared equally among all of us, which didn't amount to much, but the cigarettes were saved. They were as good as money, and sometimes even better.

One day the office was informed that a shipment of clothing donated by American Jews would soon be arriving. Eagerly we anticipated this shipment. All our garments were wearing out, and we badly needed new ones. We cleaned two rooms and were ready when the big boxes finally arrived. The workers had the privilege of choosing first. On the day of choosing, I was disappointed to find that many dresses were in very bad shape. I wondered what kind of people the donors thought we were. However, we were all glad to have something warm. I chose one green jumper, a blouse, and a sweater. This I wore for a long time. The sweater kept me warm during the whole winter.

Days became short and it was cold and impossible to spend time outside. It helped to be occupied. We workers had the obligation to go to the office, even if there was not much we could do there. But this forced us to maintain discipline and get out of the barracks. We returned to our room for lunch, then went back to the office in the afternoon. In the evening, our group frequently met in the mess hall and occasionally we even had a party. An old, hand-operated record player from JOINT headquarters was used for music, and we danced. Sometimes the JOINT officers, who were Jewish American soldiers appointed to help our camp, attended too, and were just as happy as we were to have a party. They were far away from home and were eager to be around fellow Jews. I especially liked one of these officers, and the feeling must have been mutual, for he asked me to dance often. Once a contest for best dancers was organized, and we won first place.

Life continued, and even in camps, the natural tendency to form a family was strong. Once our entire camp was invited to a wedding. Preparations started for the big event, and everybody helped make it special for the bride and groom. They had no family of their own, so we camp members acted as their family. On Friday before the wedding, a rabbi from Frankfurt came and conducted Shabbat services, a traditional blessing of the young couple. All the next day the bride was guarded from the groom's eyes. When sunset fell and the first star appeared in the darkening sky, a huppah—wedding canopy—was brought to the plaza. Next came the groom, and finally the bride, accompanied by the women. They circled the groom under the canopy seven times, according to Orthodox custom, and the

In the displaced persons camp in Babenhausen, 1945: Hanna (front row, second from left) and Kazik (second from right) with friends in front the monument erected as a memorial to prisoners who died in the Holocaust.

Hannah and friend in front of the tents in the Babenhausen camp, 1945.

marriage ceremony took place. We danced and sang, celebrating the joyful wedding. In the background stood the monument and the empty tents, silent reminders of those spirits who were witnessing a wedding and rejoicing at the beginning of a new family.

Weeks later another young couple brought a big event to the camp—the birth of a baby. During the long hours of waiting for the baby's arrival, the whole camp was on guard and took care of the nervous father-to-be. Finally a smiling nurse emerged from the clinic. "Mazel tov! It's a boy!" she exclaimed. "The mother and baby are fine!" This was a very happy occasion for all of us. This child was a symbol of the continuation of our people, a reassurance of life. On the eighth day, a rabbi came to perform a bris. After this religious ceremony, we celebrated the event with wine. In soil mixed with the ashes of our dead people, life of our new generation was born.

Near Munich in the little town of Feldafing was a large refugee camp which had been liberated by the American army. The majority of freed prisoners stayed there until arrangements could be made for them. They organized a broad spectrum of social activities and began hosting different Jewish organizations, including the Bund. As a Bundist, Father was excited about meeting friends from Bund in order to explore the possibilities of our emigration to the United States. He sold a few packages of cigarettes and bought a ticket to go by train to Munich and then to Feldafing. To his delight, when he arrived he found two friends from Łódź. They informed him there was a central refugee committee in Munich. When he returned to Munich he found the Jewish quarters, known as "Jewish Land," where Jewish activities blossomed. Even a newspaper was printed there. Father found this was not the right place for processing visas to America. He was told that in Stuttgart the Jewish Workers Committee (Bund) had a delegate, a Ms. Gould from New York, in the American consulate. Father contacted her, registered for our emigration, and requested proper documents for our transfer to a camp in Stuttgart. With this accomplished, he returned to Babenhausen.

That evening we held a family council. Mother, Kazik, and I decided that it would be good to move to Stuttgart because we'd have a better chance for emigration. It would also facilitate communication with Father's brother in America, George. For Mrs. Mess, this was a blow. She had nobody to lean on and no prospect of obtaining affidavits essential for getting a visa because she had no living relative anywhere. We didn't know what to do. Our consciences wouldn't permit us to abandon her. On the other hand, we had to do what was possible to go ahead with our lives. As we were sitting in despair, the young couple with whom Mrs. Mess had become so close came asking for permission to participate in this discussion. "We have no family," the husband said, "and our baby has no grandmother. If Mrs. Mess agrees to adopt us as her children, she can stay with us, eventually emigrate to Palestine with us, and be part of our family." Mrs. Mess was overwhelmed and did not hesitate to accept this proposition. Pieces of broken families were put together in the best possible way. Nothing could replace the loss of loved ones, but by helping each other, survivors found the strength to continue living.

I remember one very unpleasant incident that occurred in this camp. One morning I was awakened by an unusual commotion outside our barracks, then a terrible, piercing scream. We all ran outside and saw people running toward a small circle of men who kept pummeling a man who was in the center of the group. He screamed for mercy, but more and more blows fell on him. We learned that this man was recognized as a *kapo*, a German collaborator in a concentration camp, where he beat and tortured inmates. Camp security arrived and he was taken away.

Shortly after this episode, in the middle of November, our camp received an unexpected visitor. The Central Zionist Committee invited David Ben-Gurion to encourage emigration to Palestine. I remember him as a man of short stature, his white hair flying in the wind, with kind eyes. He stood on a chair so he could be seen by everyone. In his speech he assured us that soon there would be Jewish statehood. "It won't be easy," he said, "but with courage, determination, and patience, we will have our own country. I would like to see all of us in Eretz Israel. Now the British government prevents Jewish emigration to Palestine, but we will fight and we will win and we will have our Jewish land."

He left an everlasting impression on me. But his powerful speech and our expectations of a quick solution were shattered by our powerlessness in our present situation. We were a tired people with no country to call home. Nevertheless, that evening, like every Saturday after sunset, the Zionist group lit a bonfire and danced the hora and sang Hebrew songs. As the flame of the fire illuminated the darkness, the flame of hope illuminated the soul. I was sorry I did not belong to this group.

We began to plan our move to Stuttgart, delighted with the prospect of living in a city. It was decided that Father would go first in order to find housing. He arrived at the Jewish quarters and registered as a refugee from Poland. No lodgings were available for us there, in fact, not even for him, and he was told there was no shelter for the night. As evening approached, he stopped a stranger on the street and asked for help to find a hotel or room. The man listened to Father and without hesitation offered a place in his apartment. Deeply touched, Father accepted the invitation with gratitude.

The man's name was Mr. Greisendorf. He and his wife and two young sons lived in a very small apartment and shared it with Mr. Greisendorf's brother and his wife. In their crowded apartment they found space for one more. They were from Vilna and had survived the death camp in Ponary. After the war they escaped from Poland and were hoping to emigrate to America. Father was forever thankful to this extraordinary family who shared their food and lodging with a total stranger. We developed a deep friendship with this family, even after they emigrated to Canada.

The next day Father began searching for accommodations for us outside the Jewish quarters. He met a young man from Łódź, a survivor of a death camp, who eagerly offered to find something for us in return for a fair amount of German marks or cigarettes. Father paid him the requested amount of cigarettes, but unfortunately the young man disappeared without a trace. It is hard to understand, even now, that after everything we'd all been through, one Jew could do something like that to a fellow Jew.

It took Father a whole week until he found an address in a suburb of Stuttgart, on Zufenhousen Street, where one room in the home of a German family was available. Then he returned for us and we made ready to leave Babenhausen. I had a small farewell party and again said goodbye to friends whom I knew I'd not see again. Our decision to leave caused one of my friends to make the choice to return to Poland. He said he could no longer wander from country to country, with no place to call home. This was yet another difficult parting for me. I never heard of him again and do not know what happened to him.

We returned our camp belongings and packed our meager possessions. For the trip, we were given several packs of American cigarettes, which amounted to a small fortune. We boarded a train for Stuttgart.

18
STUTTGART

The city of Stuttgart lies in the midst of hills spotted with forests, orchards, vineyards, and beautiful gardens. It is approximately 120 kilometers northwest of Munich and covers both banks of the Neckar River. There are old castles, museums, Gothic buildings, and one of the most beautiful squares in Germany. The city was heavily bombed, and as we entered a year and a half after the war ended, we saw ruins and destruction everywhere, in spite of the intensive reconstruction work under way.

We arrived early in the afternoon and found a bus to take us to Zufenhousen Street. This part of town remained intact with rows of nice houses, each one built in the Gothic style as ordered by Hitler. We had no difficulty locating ours. The owner of the house, Mr. Wetzel, who was an engineer, opened the door and showed us to our room on the third floor. The first floor was occupied by a German couple with a three-year-old little boy. Mr. Wetzel and his wife lived on the second floor. The stairs led to the last landing, ending in a small hall with three separate rooms—one for us and two for a young woman and her six-year-old son. We shared a kitchen and bathroom. Everything was painted in very light colors and the whole house was clean and pleasant. Our tiny room had only the most necessary furnishings, but they occupied most of the space. There was a bed for my parents, a small bed for me, a sofa large enough for Kazik, and a small table and chairs. A window overlooking the street made the room bright and airy. We unpacked our bags and sat around the table, enjoying the almost forgotten luxury of privacy and just being the four of us again.

In order to obtain ration cards we had to register at the police precinct in a special office for refugees. After this was accomplished, it was necessary to register in the Jewish community center. To avoid infiltration of any undesired elements, each newcomer was greeted by a rabbi who asked some questions about the Jewish religion and traditions. Father had no problem in answering them, but the rest of us did. Father helped us and we were able to pass the test. It reminded me of the interrogation in Vienna, except that now our explanation was accepted and we were issued certificates stating that we belonged to the Jewish community. Based on this, we received extra ration cards from the provision office and the necessary help to pay our rent.

It was wonderful to live in a house again. Jewish life was concentrated in the Jewish quarters, where most of the refugees lived and where offices, a clinic, and a kitchen were located, and we depended upon them entirely. Small businesses like a kosher bakery, a dress and alteration shop, and many others flourished there. There were cultural programs, too, such as concerts with Jewish songs, or poetry readings in the evenings. These events were well attended and received with great enthusiasm, gratitude, and spirited applause because the audience was eager for a short respite from everyday problems. Education was not neglected and an ORT (vocational school) was established. A local militia kept watch for order and the protection of the community and prevented the entrance of unwanted elements.

In spite of efforts to sustain morale and the spirit and vitality of Jewish life, the very existence of each displaced person was demoralizing. Frustrating efforts to obtain visas to any country, lack of work, overcrowded lodging, and long lines for three free meals a day contributed to depression. We were no exceptions. Mother was in bad shape, Kazik was deteriorating fast, and Father desperately tried not to fall victim himself.

We adjusted to our new life. Our landlord treated us very well, offering his services, and even sometimes brought us a bottle of wine from his own brewery. His wife also tried to win our favors so we would give her a pack of American cigarettes. The couple on the first floor, in contrast, were hostile and avoided any conversation or contact with us because we were Jewish. The young woman who lived on our floor was pleasant. Her son was in school and we didn't see him often. She worked during the day, and in the evening after her son went to bed she entertained American soldiers in the seclusion of her room. It was not surprising that she accumulated quite a stock of American cigarettes and chocolate bars, which she kept in the kitchen cabinets.

During conversations with Mr. Wetzel, we learned that he had served in the army as a foot soldier, which was unusual, since by being an engineer he should have been an officer. We asked why, and he told us that he had rented an apartment to a Jewish doctor, which was against Nazi law, and for this infraction he was demoted to the lower rank. He served in occupied Poland but denied any awareness of atrocities. Every German we ever spoke to denied knowledge of concentration camps and Nazi criminal activities.

After weeks without anything to do, Father volunteered for any work in UNRRA. He was accepted as a tool stocker in ORT, the Jewish trade school, where Mr. Greisendorf was a teacher. Before beginning work Father had to be inoculated again, and the shots caused him to have a high fever and a swollen arm for several days. For this work he was granted some privileges and a few packages of American cigarettes. Mother took the responsibility of bringing meals from the Jewish quarter's kitchen. She had to go there by bus and carry the food home in containers.

I met a girl from Łódź and, through her, other young people. Kazik joined us, and our group became very good friends. There was absolutely nothing to occupy our time and we were all restless and demoralized. We found that Stuttgart had a technical college and institute for art, music, architecture, and agriculture, and we decided to try to enroll there. We discussed our possibilities.

"How can I go to classes," I asked, "without speaking German?"

"You will learn, just like the rest of us," was the unanimous response of my friends. "It will be better than doing nothing."

We presented our plan to JOINT and UNRRA, and they were willing to help us with tuition and transportation. Because of heavy Allied bombing that destroyed the school building, the school had been moved to a neighboring town, which required a one-hour commuter train ride. We went to the school and registered and were accepted. Each of us chose different classes. I was attracted to beginning architecture courses, with emphasis on mathematics.

Even though it was the end of November and the semester was almost over, we started attending classes anyway, partly in order to familiarize ourselves with the new environment. In the mornings we'd meet at the train station and ride together. At noon lunch was provided at a private house for a small payment. I remember sitting in a dark room at a long table with a white tablecloth and eating delicious German meals. A chubby middle-aged woman who wore an apron with a bow tied at her waist served us steaming plates of stew, cabbage with sausages, potato salad, fresh bread with butter, and sweets for dessert. Sometimes, if I close my eyes, I can almost smell the aroma of that fine food. Perhaps it was magnified after the monotony of American canned food.

After lunch, classes resumed for another two hours. I couldn't understand a word of the lectures, or the mathematical equations, and I certainly couldn't communicate with classmates. But we attended classes every day. It was a good feeling, this pursuit of accomplishment. In the middle of December winter vacation freed us until the first days of January.

By this time, a group of us had formed friendships. Special credit is due to these friends who had struggled alone since they were young children. Not only did they have the courage to survive concentration camps, hiding, and all the tragedy in their lives, they had the determination to obtain an education.

With our more permanent address, contact with Uncle George was established and, through him, with Marie and her family. We learned they were still waiting in Stockholm for visas to the United States. Meantime, George, together with Mr. Milman, an old friend of Father's who had emigrated to the United States at the beginning of the war, combined their efforts to get us out of Germany. They were informed that in New York, through a rabbi named Shapiro, for a substantial amount of money DPs could obtain visas to Cuba.

"Would you consider accepting this offer?" George asked in his letter.

"Yes! Anyplace, and as soon as possible," was our answer. Unfortunately, our excitement didn't last long.

"The project fell through," George wrote us. "The Cuban government has denied entrance to refugees." At this point we all wondered if any country would let us in. And if not, what would happen to all the people no country was willing to accept?

In the middle of this upset, I developed a high fever, severe toothache, and a swollen face. The clinic in the Jewish quarters gave me the name and address of a German dentist in the city, and Mother accompanied me to his office. The last time I had seen a dentist was before the war, more than seven years past. Many of my teeth had cavities; some were cracked, with only the root remaining inside my gums, which brought frequent infections. There were no antibiotics, and penicillin could only be obtained in an American military hospital and was treasured as much as gold. Infections were difficult to combat. I was in pain, and scared.

When the dentist sat me in his chair and asked me to open my mouth, I panicked. "Just let me take a look at your teeth," he said. "I will not hurt you." Reluctantly I submitted to his examination. "It looks bad," he said, "and you need a lot of work. But with patience, you will be fine."

I was scheduled for an appointment, at which time he would extract the first of many teeth. When I arrived at his office, I was shaking with fear. I sat in the chair and tried to convince myself that, after all, I was no longer a child, and rotten teeth had to be removed. But to no avail. The minute the dentist's hand appeared with a syringe, I closed my mouth and covered it with both my hands. A terrible thought crossed my mind—I would bite the dentist. Mother tried to talk to me; the dentist softly tried to calm me. He told me that I would be free of pain after the shot. "These bad teeth have to come out," he told me. "It is the only way to free you of these continuous infections." Finally I closed my eyes and opened my mouth. It took many visits to this dentist and a great deal of pain and discomfort before my mouth healed. Even after the infected teeth were removed and all cavities were filled, problems with my gums persisted, to this very day. I have lost almost all my own teeth.

One morning at the end of December we were awakened by a scream and a terrible cry from the child downstairs. Then we heard people running and a car leaving the house in a hurry. Father went to investigate. He returned to tell us there had been a bad accident. The woman was carrying boiling water for the weekly wash when her baby ran in front of her. She lost her balance and spilled boiling water on the child. They rushed the badly burned baby to the hospital. The whole house was worried about the little boy. Late that afternoon we learned that sixty percent of his little body was burned. In those days not too much could be done for such extensive damage.

After a week, it appeared that he was responding to treatment, but a few days later, his burns became infected. Doctors suggested that penicillin would help, but it was not yet on the market. In distress, the parents turned to us. "Please save our only child," they pleaded. "You can obtain penicillin through the Jewish authorities from the American hospital."

"I will do anything to help," Father responded. He went to the clinic in the Jewish quarters and explained the situation to the director.

"We have such small amounts of penicillin that it is impossible to provide for every need," the director said. "If we have to choose between saving a Jewish child or a German child, we will save a Jewish child. I wish I could help you, but I am sorry, I cannot."

Father returned empty handed and told the grief-stricken parents that penicillin was not available. They were furious with Father and blamed us for their misfortune. Their baby died a few days later.

Shortly afterwards, taking advantage of beautiful weather, our group decided to go to the park. In order to get there we had to take buses. We were standing in the rear of the bus, talking. In those days it was customary to leave seats for older passengers. As the bus pulled away from one of the stops it made a sudden sharp move and we lost our balance. It so happened that I ended in the arms of a young man I particularly liked. Taking advantage of the funny situation, our friends began to joke and laugh. At that moment we heard loud voices. "Look at them! It is a shame Hitler didn't finish with all the Jews. There are still too many here!"

Everyone in the bus looked at us. We ceased laughing and looked at each other. The same thought crossed our minds: "Will this ever stop?"

In the last days of December a letter from George arrived. "I was able to get in touch with a rabbi who promised to obtain visas to Mexico," he wrote. "Would you accept this offer?" Of course our answer was yes. George and Mr. Milman went to see the rabbi, who requested a deposit of one thousand dollars to facilitate the procedure. After the failure of the Cuban visas, George hesitated to hand such an enormous amount of money to a stranger who didn't even have a permanent address. The rabbi suggested that Mr. Milman hold the money, and George agreed to this. The rabbi took our personal data and another period of anxious waiting began.

To celebrate the New Year, we held a little party in our room. Each of us brought food from the mess hall, and someone got hold of a bottle of wine. We toasted and welcomed 1947 with wishes and hopes for a new life and permanent home. But for many of us, nothing was visible.

In January one more attempt was made at the American Embassy to obtain visas for us. But the person in charge of emigration was rude and hostile to Jews. He gave the standard answer: "Polish quotas are closed. No more visas will be issued this year."

Our group returned to school for the second semester. The days became longer as spring approached. On a day in April a letter from Paris arrived. Mother opened it and just sat down looking at the sheet of paper. She was speechless. Father anxiously picked it up and started to read aloud. "The Mexican Embassy acknowledges that visas for the Davidson family have arrived."

For a first few moments we were silent. Then we hugged each other as tears ran down our cheeks. Our departure from Europe was a reality, and it was overwhelming. That we would finally be allowed to emigrate was very difficult to believe. We performed our daily tasks mechanically, only half-believing that our dream of so many years would materialize. To pick up the visas it was necessary to go to Paris, because Germany did not have a Mexican embassy. Before leaving Germany, we needed valid identifications, which could be obtained in the general offices of the American army in Frankfurt. Father went to Frankfurt and obtained a family passport valid for traveling from Germany to Paris to Mexico. Then he registered in the JOINT office and placed our names on the list of emigrants with valid visas. From this point, JOINT took care of the refugees' needs, which included our transit to Paris.

We bought one heavy suitcase which would hold all our belongings and a portfolio of real leather to hold our documents. These Father paid for with American cigarettes. We were ready for the trip. We had imagined ourselves in New York, where we had family and friends, not in the wild country of Mexico, with horses and cowboys in the streets, which is what our limited information suggested. I was

Office of the Military Governor № 101677

U. S. Zone of Germany

CERTIFICATE OF IDENTITY IN LIEU OF PASSPORT

1 67
"Kennkarte" No. W B 10577
Polizei Praesidium Stuttga

Szymon D A V I D S O N
(name in full)

at Olszany   Wilna   Poland
(town)   (district)   (country)

on   3   of October   1891   male   Polish
(day)   (month)   (year)   (sex)   (citizenship)

Sofie (nee GUTENTAG)   intends to emigrate to
(given & maiden name of wife, if applicable)

M E X I C O
(country of immigration)

He (she) will be accompanied by   wife SOFIE, born 13Oct, 1893, Lodz, Poland

family members, with   daughter HANNA, born 22 Sept, 1928, Lodz, Poland
name, children and date and

son KAZIMIERZ ORZECHOWSKI, born 26 July,
1920
in Lodz, Poland

3. His (her) occupation is book-keeper

4. DESCRIPTION

Height 5 ft 7 inches

Hair grey Eyes grau

Distinguishing marks or features:

(signature of applicant)

5. He (she) solemnly declares that he (she) has never committed nor has he (she) been
convicted of any crime except as follows

no exceptions

6. He (she) is unable to produce birth certificates, marriage license, divorce papers
and / or police record for the following reasons

All papers have been destroyed during the war and the deportation.

7. I hereby certify that the description o the person(s) whose photograph(s) is affixed
hereto is correct and that he (she, they) declare(s) that the facts stated above are true.

(signature of applicant)

Signed 13 . March . 47
(day)   (month)   (year)

at   Frankfurt.
(location)

(signature of certifying officer)

Chief Processing Center Section
DP Branch, G-5 USFET
(position)

Certificate of identity issued to the Davidson family in lieu of passport, March 13, 1947. All family papers had been destroyed during the war.

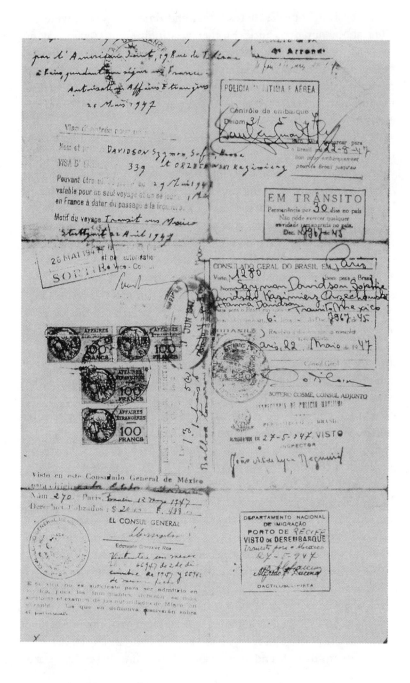

Reverse of the certificate of identity with visas of countries on route to Mexico.

apprehensive about life there. Father and Kazik, however, were excited about our departure. Mother was indifferent. Again, saying goodbye to my friends was very difficult this time, especially the young man who was my special friend. When we parted, he hugged me tightly and looked into my eyes. "It is a miracle that such a trusting and innocent creature survived the war," he said softly. "I will remember you."

We parted in the evening. All four of my friends would stay in Germany and continue their education as long as JOINT would sponsor them. Two would go into medicine, one into biology, and one into engineering. In the cool April night, the door closed as they left and disappeared from my view. I lost all contact with them as we moved from one place to another, and I never heard from them again. I often think of them as fine professionals settled in some corner of the world. I miss all the friends I left behind.

We said an emotional farewell to the Greisendorfs. Our landlord, Mr. Wetzel, took us to the bus station in his car, and our friends saw us off with tears and flowers. On the bus, we looked out the window and waved our last goodbyes.

In a few hours the UNRRA bus arrived in Frankfurt and took us directly to JOINT offices, where we were issued French transit visas and given financial aid for our trip and stay in Paris. The next three days we spent in an UNRRA camp, waiting for our departure. It was there that I found the sister of my schoolmate and best friend, Stefcia. She told us that her parents did not survive the concentration camps, and she told us how she parted with Stefcia and of her terrible death. I couldn't stop crying.

When we were finally cleared for departure, we boarded a train to Paris, which was very exciting. Traveling in a Pullman coach was a long-forgotten experience—the past seven years we had traveled only in boxcars, cattle trains, trucks, or by walking. Sitting by a window and watching the landscape change was wonderful.

We shared our compartment with a young woman who told us she was going to Paris on her way to Algiers. She told us her story. While she was working on a German farm, she became friends with a Polish girl and showed us a photograph of the two of them. Mother looked at the photo and recognized the Polish girl as Dosia, her student and my dear friend from school, but some habits die hard indeed. Accustomed as we were to living in fear of compromising a friend, we did not reveal that we knew her. Mother did mention that this girl reminded her of someone. "If by any chance you see this girl again," Mother said, "please tell her if the name Davidson is familiar to her, we will be registered at JOINT."

Early in the evening we reached the German and French borders. A French official entered our compartment and checked our documents. As he stamped them, he nodded to me and said, "Bon voyage, bon nuit."

The comfortable accommodations and monotonous sound of the train were very soothing, and I slept, dreaming about Paris. The next morning Mother woke me. "We'll be in Paris soon," she said. "Look. The city is there."

19
PARIS

I was on my feet immediately. The suburbs were visible now, small houses were replaced by big ones, and soon we entered the city. The train stopped at the Gare du Nord Station. It had been a long and difficult journey from the remote and primitive forest of a Russian kolkhoz to the streets of Paris. It did not seem real to me.

Paris greeted us with a gray drizzle the April morning we arrived. A JOINT employee waited for our small group and escorted us by bus to its office building. After we registered, we were given the address of a hotel in which we'd be staying until our departure for Mexico. Coupons for dinners in assigned restaurants were given to us, as were other coupons to buy products for breakfast and lunch. We were also given pocket money. The order with which JOINT handled the masses of wandering survivors is truly amazing.

My parents spoke French, so we ventured to the hotel on our own. After awhile the streets began to narrow, the houses looked unkempt and not very appealing, small shops were crowded with unsmiling people. This old section of the city was called in Yiddish "Pletzel," meaning "little place," and until the war had been predominantly Jewish. Many of the Paris Jews perished in concentration camps during the war.

We finally found our hotel. It was four stories high with one window per floor. It was built when only aristocracy could have spacious houses and burghers had to build their homes with facades only three meters wide. The front door opened to a dark reception space leading to old wooden stairs that had been painted red many years ago. Only traces of red were visible. The stairs were so worn out that stepping in the middle could cause breakage. It was necessary to press one's body closely next to the rail or the wall to climb them.

We reached the second-floor hall and to our shock found a completely naked prostitute in front of us. She was absolutely unconcerned about our presence there. My parents turned white, my face turned red, and my brother's eyes nearly popped out. Only when we recovered a bit did we dare to open the door to our room.

The room had been painted pink at some time but now the walls were of indeterminate gray color and they were completely dotted with squashed bedbugs. One small bed occupied the whole room. The bedding and linens, once white, were now gray rags. There was a tiny, dirty window and a bare lightbulb hanging from the ceiling, cobwebs in the corners, and one rusty wash basin. At the end of the hall was one very dirty bathroom used by the whole floor. There was a metal stand with a hole in the middle and marks for feet to step on when in use. Father and Kazik shared a room while Mother and I shared the adjacent one. I wondered if JOINT was aware of the rundown condition of the quarters they had assigned to us.

The effects of the war were visible everywhere. Food was rationed, buildings were dilapidated, and people were depressed. There was a general bleakness in the air. This part of town was not the Paris I had imagined—this was the Paris of the poor.

Early in the morning there was a knock on the door. We opened it and there stood Dosia, the girl Mother had recognized in the photograph on the train. Sobbing, she threw herself into Mother's arms and could not stop crying for a long, long time. Overwhelmed with emotion, she told us her story. "I lost my parents and my whole family," she said. "I lost everything from the world of yesterday. It was as if I ceased to exist. I was totally alone. You are the only person in the world who knows my past." To be in the arms of the only person she had found who was a link to her past, to her parents, was unbelievable to her. The powerful impact of this scene haunts me even now.

There were thousands of refugees in Paris awaiting emigration. The biggest problem was the lack of transportation. Even with our Mexican visas we had to wait for transportation, hoping that our visas wouldn't expire. Boats and planes were booked for months in advance.

While in Paris I found a friend from Łódź. He survived with his parents and, like the rest of us, was waiting for emigration. We got together and with another fellow decided to explore the city. It was a beautiful spring in Paris. We were young and full of energy. We climbed the Eiffel Tower, we ran through the incredible gardens at Versailles where we managed to steal a kiss or two, we admired the Louvre—even though the art treasures were still packed from being evacuated during the war—and we visited Montmartre. We attended an impressive mass in the Cathedral of Notre Dame. We traveled in the Parisian metro, where more kisses were exchanged. We strolled along the tree-lined Champs-Élysées enjoying ourselves, forgetting for a time our worries and anxiety. Lack of money didn't affect us. We were in Paris, the city of love, beauty was in the air, and our youthful freedom was intoxicating.

I didn't notice the condition of our hotel anymore, or mind the meals in assigned restaurants with multilingual crowds, deafening noise, and not very attractive food. I had spread my wings and I was flying.

However, the reality of our situation was not so bright as my illusion of it. Days and weeks went by with no solution to the problem of transportation. Our visas were valid only until the first of June 1947, and it was already the middle of May. The tension, impatience, and inactivity were unbearable. In desperation Father sought help through a connection with ORT, but with no result. "We'll do whatever is possible," he was told, "but there is no transportation." At this point we almost lost our hope for a future of any kind.

About this time a Bund international convention was held in Brussels with delegations from every Bund organization. The delegation from Mexico was in Paris on the way to Brussels. From them we obtained information about Mexico, but they could do nothing to help with our transportation. "Here is a telephone number of Mr. Z in Mexico," Father was told. "Call him when you arrive." But only ten days remained until our visas expired.

We were not alone in this absolutely helpless situation. My friend was waiting to go to Australia, and others were trying to leave Paris for any country to which they could obtain visas. There simply was not enough transportation to accommodate everybody. Dosia had a relative in the United States who promised to help her. While she waited, she obtained work in the Pasteur Institute. We were with her every day and every minute we could be.

The end of May came. Spring was almost gone, and the beauty of Paris was fading. Depression crept over us all. Then a lucky and unexpected accident changed our situation. By chance, while walking down a street, Father met a friend from Łódź. It was always emotional to find someone who had survived. As they told each other their stories of surviving, Father told his friend about our problem. "Davidson," the man said, "I know a travel agency that will get you passage to Mexico. I did this already for two other families from Łódź." Father did not know if JOINT would pay for passage provided by private enterprise but had nothing to lose by asking. They went together to the JOINT office and presented the plan. To our indescribable happiness, the proposal was accepted. At long last we had a real prospect of ending our years of suffering, homelessness, and living on charity. There was a problem, however. We could not get reservations for a flight from Paris to Mexico City via New York. We had to fly a roundabout way: To Portugal, then change planes for Brazil via Dakar, change planes again for another South American country, and finally for Mexico. But we only had a week left on our visas.

JOINT provided the tickets for our trip and $140 American for expenses and helped us obtain transit visas from the Brazilian embassy. We would obtain other visas later in Brazil. We got tickets to Mexico, but we didn't know the day or the hour of our arrival there.

It was very difficult to say goodbye to my friends, especially to Dosia. I had mixed feelings about leaving her in Paris. On one hand, I was glad that we'd be on our way to a new place, a new life in a new home. On the other hand, I felt guilty about my luck and good fortune while the rest of my friends were still without transportation. Our departure was heartbreaking and tearful. They insisted on seeing us off, so we all packed into a taxi and went to Orly Airport. As we passed through customs I turned for a last wave. All of us were crying at this last painful goodbye.

We proceeded to an airplane. My feet were weak and I was trembling as we were about to board. Until this moment I had associated airplanes as a means of bombs, air raids, destruction, not as a method of transportation. I think we all felt this, because we slowed our walk toward the plane. Father decided to be the brave one and give us courage, so he stepped ahead of us to show us it was all right to board. He was quickly held back by the steward, however. "Les dames premier, s'il vous plait," he said. Ladies first. He then helped Mother and me as we climbed the steps. Father and Kazik had to climb on their own.

As we entered the cabin we saw plush seats, two on each side of a carpeted isle. We would be flying on a new plane, a DC-4, which Kazik assured me was safer than the DC-3s that had recently crashed. Well-dressed passengers contrasted with our ill-fitting and shabby clothing, but we didn't let this bother us. The engine roared, the plane moved, and we felt ourselves leaving the ground as the plane ascended. As the airport disappeared from view, I saw my friends standing below, watching our plane become only a dot in the sky, just as I was watching them. I felt the enormity of the distance, of the separation. When I couldn't see anything but blue, I closed my eyes and engraved the last sight of my past. Poland, Russia, Germany, France, and all of Europe melted behind us.

20
FLIGHT TO MEXICO

Our first stop was in Lisbon, Portugal, for refueling. When we left Lisbon, our flight was so smooth it was difficult to tell the plane was in motion. We savored the splendid dinner served on a tray which was covered with a white napkin. Later I fell asleep, resting my head on a soft pillow and covered with a warm blanket. I did not wake until we landed in Dakar to prepare for crossing the Atlantic on the way to Recife, Brazil, which was the shortest distance between these two continents.

It was completely dark when we descended from the plane and entered the airport. After formalities, all passengers were invited to a hall. As we entered we saw a long table covered with a white cloth filled with beautifully decorated trays of fruit, snacks, cheese, crackers, bread, meat, fish, and an endless assortment of mouth-watering pastries. Passengers gathered around the table, chatting and piling plates with all the goodies. I reached for a plate, but Father stopped me. "Don't eat," he said. "We cannot afford this. It probably costs a fortune." I stepped aside, but my mouth watered as my eyes devoured the food. Two hours later we boarded our plane. It was only then that we learned the food was courtesy of Air France.

We crossed the Atlantic during the night. A few hours after taking off, we entered a heavy thunderstorm. Lightning illuminated the cabin, thunder was louder than the propellers, and some of the passengers, including Kazik, became sick. I covered my head with a blanket, which helped ease my anxiety. After this long night we watched the sun rise in a bright, cloudless sky. As the shores of South America appeared below us, it was difficult to grasp the enormous distance that we covered in just a matter of hours. We were used to walking and covering but a few kilometers in the same time span.

A hot, humid breeze greeted us as we disembarked from the plane at Recife. We proceeded to customs, amazed at the intense heat, palm trees, and the large variety of flowers. This sudden transformation from our European climate to the tropics of South America was incredible. Fortunately, we passed all formalities quickly. In those times, traveling by plane was considered a luxury, and passengers were treated accordingly. Even our shabby clothing was ignored.

Not anticipating any difficulties, we went to a ticket counter to confirm our flight out of Recife. To our horror we found that all flights were full. We had to wait three days for the next available seats, which would take us to Fortaleza, Brazil, with the possibility of connection to Mexico City. Meantime the validity of our visas was running out.

We had to find a hotel. Since we did not speak Portuguese, we used sign language to communicate with a taxi driver and requested that he take us to an inexpensive hotel. Instead, he thought we were tourists and drove us to a very fancy one. The rooms were elegant: luxurious bathrooms that one could enjoy in complete privacy, soft beds with clean white linen, rugs, tables and chairs, large windows with draperies. What a change from the hotel in Paris only twenty-hours ago! We even went to a restaurant for our first meal on the American continent. But we were very concerned about this tremendous expense at the beginning of our trip, a trip that was to take much longer than we anticipated.

The hotel was located in the business section. When we ventured out, we were struck by streets lined with palm trees, stores with doors wide open, loud music blasting from inside, offering good Brazilian coffee to everyone who entered. We couldn't understand the language but accepted the coffee. The heat was suffocating by now, and we were just about to return to the hotel when we passed a furniture store. Father decided to go in. He began to speak Yiddish and to our amazement, the man behind the counter answered in Yiddish. From him we learned that Recife was home to about five hundred Jews and that JOINT had a branch located there.

Later that afternoon there was a knock on our hotel room door. I opened it and two volunteers from the ladies' auxiliary of the JOINT committee entered. The news had spread quickly in the Jewish community that the first Holocaust survivors had reached the city. The ladies came to welcome us with flowers and gifts. We were offered any help we might need and were invited into their homes. Father was offered a teaching position so children could learn Yiddish. They wanted to know everything about the Polish Jews, about the Holocaust, first hand. All of them came from Poland before World War I, and now they listened to us in distress, sobbing openly. Many lost families in Europe.

One woman introduced herself. "I am from Łódź," she said. "I came here alone and never had a chance to go back, but your name sounds familiar to me."

"I knew your family very well," Father exclaimed. "I am sorry to tell you that on our return to Poland, I learned that they all perished in a concentration camp." Her response was very emotional. When she recovered somewhat, she reminisced about her younger years and talked about people she had known.

On Saturday, our last day in Recife, we were invited to a wedding that took place at the Jewish community center. All Jewish families participated in the celebration of this happy occasion. When the ceremony began, beautiful music ushered in exquisitely dressed little boys and girls. They were followed by bridesmaids escorted by young men. Parents escorted the groom to the huppah, which was covered with flowers. The nuptial march began to play and a little girl entered, throwing rose petals on the carpet. The bride followed, walking on the roses. Her dress was made of delicate lace and tulle and silk and had a long train. She was holding a most splendid bouquet of white flowers. Her head and face were covered with a veil, but I could see that she was very young, no more than sixteen. It was difficult to believe that this scene was real and not a theater performance.

After the religious ceremony, a banquet was served and an orchestra played while people ate and danced. Kazik was quickly invited to participate, but I was ignored. Father had been greatly encouraged to make a permanent home here. He was assured that he, and especially Kazik, would have excellent futures in Recife. Young single men were highly desired—young single women were not.

We learned that festivities like this one were customary in prosperous Jewish communities across the Americas. I could not understand and deeply resented the fact that while fellow Jews were martyred and dying during Nazi persecution, such revelries were being held, even as the suffering among the European Jews was still happening.

We left Recife on Sunday. People came to the hotel to bid us goodbye and to accompany us to the airport. We were thankful for the hospitality of the Jewish community and grateful for their warm reception and the help that they extended to us. Soon we were on our way to Fortaleza. We were glad to have a meal served on the plane, as our limited resources were shrinking and we didn't know how long it would take us to reach Mexico.

As soon as we landed in Fortaleza, we tried to arrange our next flight. The only connection available was to Belem, in northeast Brazil, with the slight possibility of being able to continue to Trinidad, Panama City, and Mexico. We had to spend the night in Fortaleza, and after we settled in a hotel, we went to see the town. Although Fortaleza was not large, it was a beautiful city with an active commercial zone. In one of the stores we passed Father asked for a postcard in Yiddish. A man answered him, also in Yiddish.

The next day we left for Belem. Since this was to be our last stop in Brazil, our visas had to be authorized there. The airport official said that we had to pay him for stamping our passports. Father refused to pay because he knew there should not be a charge for this. We contacted a travel agency and they directed us to the passport office. After an agonizing wait, a clerk came out and stamped our passports. He criticized the person who demanded money from us. "It hurts tourism," he said. "It is the same as robbery."

That evening we went to the hotel restaurant for our meal. At the entrance, we were stopped by a hostess. "You can't dine here without a jacket," she said referring to Father and Kazik.

"We don't have jackets," Kazik replied.

She looked at our shabby clothing. "We can lend you one of ours," she said. She handed two large jackets to Father and Kazik, which attracted attention to us. It was terribly embarrassing, and I wanted to run away.

Father stopped me. "I am not ashamed," he said. "We are as respectable as anyone here." With this, he walked to a table, where we ordered two of the least expensive plates on the menu and split them among the four of us.

We left Belem in the morning with Trinidad as our destination. About an hour after takeoff, the captain announced, "Ladies and gentlemen, congratulations from the crew of this ship on crossing the equator at this moment." Everybody cheered, and the stewardess brought us all champagne. Later we received an official certificate to mark the occasion.

The Trinidad airport was located far from the city, so passengers had to be transported both ways. There was a small airline hotel near the airport and we asked to stay there, as we didn't feel we could afford the cost of the one in town. This hotel, a round building with a gallery encircling it, was situated in a meadow on the edge of a rainforest. Palm trees shadowed the courtyard, and the fragrance of colorful flowers filled the air. At the entrance we were greeted by an incredibly lovely bird, a macaw, flying toward us repeating over and over again, "Welcome!" Since we were the only guests there, the manager gave us two luxuriously furnished rooms.

It was very hot, but nothing could stop us from exploring. A dirt path led to a nearby village. Sweaty, naked children with extended bellies played outside huts, along with dogs, monkeys, and other kinds of small animals. Seeing us coming, they scattered and disappeared behind huts. Vegetation was so thick and trees were so high that it was almost dark as we walked deeper and deeper into the forest. Songs of birds, noises made by monkeys and insects blended to sound like an orchestra performing a symphony of wild sounds. My thoughts returned to another place where such a short time ago I'd stood in an equally majestic forest which was covered with a thick blanket of snow where the silence was so complete, shattered only occasionally by howling wolves. I remembered shivering in that cold. Both forests, thousands of miles apart and so different in nature, were so alike in the misery and suffering of people struggling for survival.

That evening we had a splendid dinner. The table was covered with a white tablecloth, matching napkins, and a crystal vase with fresh flowers centering delicate plates and silver. We were the only diners and were served generous portions of everything and all the desserts we could eat. While we enjoyed having this abundance, we were all worried, for on this day, the first of June 1947, our visas to Mexico had expired.

We left Trinidad at noon the next day and landed that evening in Panama City. A taxi took us to the Hotel Central, a charming place in front of a beautiful plaza with a gazebo, benches, palms, and the ever-present abundant flowers. Streets were crowded with pedestrians, traffic, and stores. Again, Father found that the owner of one of the stores spoke Yiddish, and so he established communication. Panama had a substantial Jewish community, and word quickly spread that a Jewish family from Poland had arrived. As before, we were invited to the Jewish center, where people gathered to meet us. They cried as they listened to our story. They also had lost families in Europe. They invited us into their homes for meals, they showed us their city, and offered us their help.

The next day we boarded a plane for Guatemala, where we were to transfer to the Mexican airline for our final destination. We watched the tropical landscape change below us as mountains appeared on the horizon. One of these mountains was Ixtaccihuatl, and the other was Popocatepetl. A young man seated near us told us about it. "Legend has it that Popo, a warrior, is watching over his dead sweetheart," he said, "a volcano in the shape of a sleeping woman."

We approached Mexico City. I saw tall buildings, automobiles, and heavy traffic. I did not see horses on the street or Indians. We had finally reached our destination.

21
MEXICO CITY

Passengers were directed to customs at the entrance of the airport. We were all filled with anxiety as we followed the line. With every step we were closer and closer to the immigration officer. Our hearts were pounding as we wondered what would happen. When it was our turn, Father was asked for our documents. He handed them over. The inspector examined our papers and the expression on his face told us we were in trouble. He said something in Spanish, which we could not understand, and pointed to our visas. Father offered him a pack of cigarettes, which he accepted, but still held onto our visas. Our visas had expired two days before, and we would not be allowed to leave the airport. We were to be sent back.

"Back where?" Father asked.

"Back to Poland," the inspector answered.

"We can't go," Father responded. "We lost our Polish citizenship when we escaped from Poland."

"Then you must go to Germany or France," the inspector said.

"But we are not Germans or French," Father said. "We are Jews, and we have nowhere to go."

As we were taken to a back room, Mother fainted. This was more than she could endure. Father and Kazik were ashen. In absolute panic I kneeled beside Mother and held her head. An airport nurse came and helped us. When Mother recovered, she was very weak. We helped her lie down on the only wooden bench in the room.

At that point, a Yiddish-speaking man approached us and offered his assistance. He turned to Father and whispered, "Let me have your documents. I'll negotiate with the inspector." He took our papers, put money inside, and handed them to the customs official. "Please allow this family to go to a hotel for the night," he said. "The old lady is not well and needs rest." An agreement was reached. Our documents would be held, but we were permitted to leave the airport and return the next day. Once out of the airport, the Jewish community could provide us with assistance.

Father called Mr. Z, whose telephone number had been given to us in Paris. Mr. Z was president of the Mexican Bund organization. "Davidson from Łódź," Mr. Z said after Father introduced himself. "I already got information about your coming. Reservations have been made for your family in a boardinghouse. Do not worry. Everything will be fine. You will not be sent back." We took a taxi to the *pension*, or boardinghouse, where rooms, including food, were rented to tourists. The taxi dropped us in front of a two-story house, and a friendly hostess showed us to our room, which had been paid for by the Jewish community center.

The tension of the last few hours in the airport had drained all our energy. We slept well that night knowing there would be no more exile for us. The next day Father met with the Committee secretary and went to the airport. They conferred with the inspector who held our documents. "I need ten pesos for the inspector," the secretary whispered to Father.

"This is my last ten pesos," Father replied and gave it over. "We have no more money."

The inspector put the money in his pocket and with no further delay affixed the required stamps and returned our documents. This was our first lesson in how to conduct business in Latin America.

On the $140 American given to us by JOINT at the beginning of our journey, the four of us made the incredible trip through Europe, Africa, South and Central America, to arrive in Mexico. Finally, in Mexico City, our eight years of harsh existence ended. It was now time to begin rebuilding our lives. Our visas were extended with the help of the right people and with the right amount of money. However, work permits were denied. But work was essential in order for us to survive. With the help of the Jewish community, Father was hired at the level of an errand boy. He didn't complain, because he was grateful to earn any money he could. Kazik got a job as a helper in one of the shops. The only work available to me was that of a maid, and that salary would not be enough to justify the risk of being expelled from Mexico for working without a permit. There was no question of Mother working.

We settled into our new lives. As thankful as I was for my new home, I soon realized that I faced particular difficulties. As a woman, I couldn't be on the street alone after dark, which meant that I had to depend on Father or Kazik if I needed to go somewhere after sunset. And I learned that at my age, I was past being marriageable.

"Here in Mexico, girls marry young," I was informed. "At your age they already have one or two children. If you are more than sixteen or seventeen, you are considered to be an old maid. Not only are you too old, but you are poor. Sometimes with money, a marriage can be arranged. But you are a refugee and you have no money. Without a dowry, nobody will consider you for marriage." This was a terrible blow to me. I was just a teenager, but already past marriageable age and without dowry. Instead of my dreams for new friendships and a bright future, apparently I was to have none. I became depressed and cried myself to sleep at night. Eventually I decided that crying would take me nowhere, so I dried my tears and began to examine the possibilities open to me. Since education was practically free, I enrolled at the polytechnic (university), majoring in chemistry and microbiology.

I met another refugee girl from Poland, the same age as I, and we became friends. She discovered that a Jewish Zionist youth organization held meetings each month and proposed that she and I would attend these meetings. At the first meeting, we sat in the back and listened to the program. Since I was just learning Spanish, I did not understand much of the discussion. In spite of our efforts to introduce ourselves in broken Spanish, we were ignored. After the meeting, people left in groups or in pairs, and we two girls began our walk home alone. The streets were dark and empty, but we gave each other courage. We came to a corner where she had to turn left and I had to turn right. Alone, I panicked. "What have I done?" I asked myself. "I am going to be molested and killed." I was completely out of breath and my heart was beating so fast it felt like it might burst by the time I finally reached home. I didn't want to go through this ever again, but I was too proud and too stubborn to admit defeat. I went to the next meeting, but I was miserable at the gathering and petrified of coming home alone.

I knew it was dangerous, but I decided that I had to attend just one more meeting. One of the activities of the organization was to collect money to help build a Jewish state. At parties held in the Jewish community, young men and women would pair up to solicit funds. Names of girls were called out, and young men interested in a particular girl raised their hands as her name was called. When my name was called by the president of the organization, there was total silence and no hand went up. "Who wants to go with her?" the president asked.

I heard giggling and whispering, but nobody spoke for me. I was terribly embarrassed and humiliated and sorry I ever came. But I held my head high. My name was called once more.

"Well, since nobody is willing to go with her," the president said, "I guess I will have to go with her myself." He looked at me. "I will pick you up on Saturday evening."

He picked me up on the appointed Saturday, then the next Saturday, and the next. Four years later, when he finished medical school, Jaime Pankowsky and I were married.

In the meantime I attended classes. I enjoyed being at school, absorbing knowledge, accomplishing difficult tasks in the lab, and meeting new students. I became particularly close with two girls, and the three of us became best friends. Our friendship continues to this day. One is so dear to me that she is like a part of my family. The other, Sarita, became my sister-in-law when she married Kazik. Now retired, Kazik and Sarita live in Mexico City, as does their daughter, Aurora, and her son, Alan. Aurora is a physician specializing in infectious diseases, and Alan attends elementary school.

Hanna (in a dress from the displaced persons camp in Babenhausen) with husband-to-be Jaime Pankowsky, in Mexico City, 1948.

Now that we had a permanent address, we contacted George and, through him, Marie. She and the twins had arrived in New York from Stockholm on the same day that we landed in Mexico. Her husband Frank and her mother Stephany had been denied visas to enter the United States, and they remained in Sweden. In the spring of 1948, Frank was hired as a cook on a ship bound for Cuba. When the ship anchored in New York, he managed to escape and ran to the apartment where his family lived. In time, he obtained legal papers. Today Frank and Marie still live in New York. Marie, who is an artist, continues to paint. Frank retired after a successful business career and organized a movement to recognize and help the Righteous Ones, those who selflessly helped save Jewish lives. He has written a book about his war experiences, *Years at the Edge of Existence*, by Frank Morgens. The twins are both married: Anne has two boys, David and Matthew, and Sylvia has two girls, Lara and Dorian.

The Morgens family and (center front) Ala Sztajnert, during Sztajnert's visit to New York, 1961. Left to right: Frank; the twins, Anne and Sylvia, and Marie.

Stephany was forced to remain in Sweden for five lonesome years. She lost all hope of seeing her family again. "Thank you for the photos," she wrote to us. "I put them on the table to feel your presence here. I don't think I'll ever see you again."

When Marie became an American citizen, she was finally able to obtain a visa for her mother. In November of 1951, Stephany arrived in New York as an emigrant and remained there until her death in 1977.

Zev and Vala left Germany shortly after our departure. They had a long and difficult journey. They walked through the Alps until they crossed the Italian boarder illegally during the night. A Hagana car was waiting for them and transported them to facilities for Jewish refugees in Milan. Then they were moved to the town of Santa Maria di Leuca, a port on the Ionian Sea, where they stayed with a group of Hagana for a long time. Vala worked as a nurse while there. A rabbi legalized their marriage in a religious ceremony, and Vala decided to change her name. Vala, which is short for Valentyna, is a Polish name. She wanted a name which would reflect the Jewish faith she now embraced, and so choose Ala.

Their Hagana group moved later to a small port town in the hope of boarding a boat which would take them to Palestine. The boat didn't come, so they proceeded to Lodispoli, another small port. After many weeks of anxiety, a ship, *Lo Tafchidonu*, anchored at this port, and during the night and in total silence the refugees boarded the vessel. Ala wrote to us that "the only sound I heard were the waves of the ocean and the movement of the feet of Hagana fighters in the icy water as they helped people get to the ship." Their heavily overloaded boat began its voyage to Palestine but was caught in a storm. Only through enormous effort was the Italian crew able to bring the boat safely to the Palestinian shore.

During a black night, just as they were disembarking, an English patrol intercepted their boat and apprehended all the refugees. They were taken to Haifa and sent to a detention camp in Cyprus. Not one of my friends had reached Palestine, but all ended in the same detention camp. Conditions in this camp were very bad. Those incarcerated lived in misery, depression, inactivity, and helplessness.

"My loved ones," Father wrote to Ala, "it is true that we are already in place establishing our new life. In my heart I feel deep pain

Ala at the planting of her tree in Yad Vashem.

Ala's tree.

for you and all our friends, who, two and a half years after such terrible war, are still in camps. I scream over the injustice that is imposed on people, especially Jews. But I believe that this difficult period will pass. You are young. After the passing of years, when you will be established and on your own, you will remember with satisfaction this trying time when you were able to stand on your feet on solid earth. At least I do remember that I fought and I survived. I am proud of it. So you will be, too."

And they were. In August of 1948, after the State of Israel was born, they reached the promised land. Zev served in the Israeli army and fought against the enemies of the new Jewish country. In May of 1985, the Jewish nation expressed gratitude and honored Ala by asking her to plant a tree in her name in Yad Vashem, Alley of the Righteous. She received a medal with the inscription: "He who saves one life, saves the entire world" and an award as a "Righteous among the Nations." She was accorded by the Knesset, the Israeli Parliament, the title of "Honored Citizen of Israel." Zev died the last day of 1996, and one week afterward Ala slipped into a coma and passed away. She was put to rest next to her Zev in a special cemetery for the Righteous Ones. She was a petite woman, but it was said of her that she was small outside, but a giant inside, a young Polish woman who put her own life in danger to save not one but many lives. Ala's tree will be there forever in memoriam of her heroic past.

Dosia lived in Israel where she married, had two children, and six grandchildren. She died in April of 1996 and is missed by all of us who loved her.

Lilly and her husband emigrated to Uruguay. She died in a car accident several years ago, leaving behind beloved children and grandchildren.

Maryla lived in New York until her death. She had two children and several grandchildren.

Hania, her parents, and her sisters Bella and Edzia emigrated to Israel from Cyprus. She lived in Haifa with her husband Chaim. I recently received news from Israel about Hania's sudden and unexpected death. She left behind the richest legacy one can have, two sons, seven grandchildren, and four great-grandchildren, the fourth generation of survivors who will continue our heritage. Now I stand alone, the last one of my classmates.

When Jaime graduated from medical school, he had to serve for six months in a small town. He was assigned to Cuervos in Baja California. To buy groceries, we had to cross the border to an American town, Yuma. On our first trip we were stopped at the frontier village of Algodones. The border police checked our papers and gave Jaime documents permitting him to enter Yuma any time he wanted. To me, however, permission was denied. I stood on the sandy road in this remote place not believing that I would not be allowed to go to the store just a few steps away.

During the McCarthy era of the early fifties, anybody exposed to Communism was suspected of spying. Could they possibly believe that those howling wolves underneath the window of our hut in Russia were howling secrets of importance? Or was the freezing wind blowing through my bones informing me of the secrets of the forest during my walks in deep snow on my way to school? Or perhaps the murmur of icy water in the stream where I washed our clothes during the brief summer told me top state secrets. It is a fact that during the eight months I lived in Cuervos, I was never allowed to go to the grocery story in Yuma.

In July of 1952, Jaime secured a residency in surgery at Sinai Hospital in Baltimore, Maryland. I, however, was yet again denied permission to enter the United States. Even now that I was a Mexican citizen, I was still considered to be undesirable. This was very hard for me, especially since I was expecting our first child. I was forced to remain with my parents in Mexico, who welcomed me and helped me fight the terrible depression resulting from my forced separation from my husband.

22
A NEW LIFE

The Central Bund Committee petitioned in my behalf and eventually obtained a visitor's visa for me. I arrived in Baltimore late in November, and our daughter, Helen, was born in the middle of January, 1953. Once again I was to learn a new language. Polish, of course, is my native language; then I was forced to learn Russian very quickly. It didn't take me long to learn Spanish because I was in school and around students who wished to help me communicate. I learned English very slowly because I was so isolated in Baltimore. This language was my most difficult task, and I still struggle with it today. I was able to renew my visitor's visa, and our son, Danny, was born three years later. When Jaime finished his residency, we made our home in San Antonio, Texas. Jaime retired recently. Helen is a psychiatrist and lives in San Antonio with her husband, Dan, and their son, Jay. Danny is a pathologist and lives in Nashville with his wife, Susan, and their children, Nathan and Shirit.

In 1964 I was at last allowed to become an American citizen. I remember how excited and scared I was when we went before the judge for our examinations. My heart beat loudly as I answered the questions put to me. I was well prepared since I studied vigorously all the required material. The judge shook my hand and congratulated me. After so many years, I was welcome to stay in my new home. I was a legal American citizen. We celebrated this big event surrounded by our friends Norman and Edna Brown and our children. After a meal, traditional apple pie decorated with American flags was brought to our table accompanied by the song "America the Beautiful." In seconds, the whole restaurant was singing with us as joyful tears rolled down my cheeks. I'll never forget how proud I was when for the first time in my life I went to vote, conscious of my duty, my obligation, and my privilege.

In 1976 my parents became citizens of the United States. Mother continued to paint, but she was always withdrawn. She died at the age of ninety-six, leaving a legacy of paintings, some of which were deemed masterpieces by John Leeper, late director of the McNay Art Museum. Her early work, however—all the paintings, sculptures, and my beautiful butterfly—is forever lost.

At the age of eighty-three when he came to us, Father began a new and very active life. He learned English and volunteered his services to the University of Texas at San Antonio, where he started and organized a collection of Yiddish books from all over the world. This important collection of more than six thousand volumes is today a monument of Jewish culture. He wrote his memoirs, which the university published under the title *My War Years*, by Simon Davidson. He died a few weeks before his ninety-seventh birthday.

The roots of generations have been transplanted to many countries and the seeds continue to grow. The cradle of Jewish culture in Łódź was completely destroyed.

At this time in my life, I begin to fully understand the significance of the words Father wrote to Ala in 1973. I, too, remember difficult times, the difficulties imposed upon us all. I survived and am standing on solid earth. I opened the door for future generations. They are free.

Sofia Davidson with three of her paintings on the Terrace of her apartment in Mexico City, late 1960s.

Sofia Davidson at an exhibit of some of her paintings, possibly in the Jewish Community Center, Mexico City, early 1970s.

Hanna speaking to one of many San Antonio classrooms about the Holocaust, 1988.

GLOSSARY

AJJDC: American Jewish Joint Distribution Committee, a relief and welfare organization that helped Jewish refugees and displaced persons relocate to new homes during and after World War II. It worked in conjunction with other relief organizations, such as UNRRA and ORT (see below).

Bund: A major Jewish socialist party in Eastern Europe that defended Jewish cultural life and autonomy against Leninism, clashed with Russian and Polish anti-Semitic parties, and fought Jewish assimilation. It also clashed with Zionists over the necessity of establishing a separate Jewish homeland in Palestine and published anti-Zionist pamphlets and manifestos. It was despised by the communist leadership in the Soviet Union which labelled Bundists as separatists and nationalists (despite their opposition to a Jewish homeland in Palestine) and considered them to be counter-revolutionaries dedicated to overthrowing the Bolsheviks, and punishable under Article 58, points 10 and 11 of the Soviet criminal code, which made it a crime to agitate against the Soviet system in any way. The people arrested under this law are known as "political 58s" or "Politicals." Those sentenced under points 10 and 11 of the Article were sent to distant labor camps for class-dangerous elements requiring a more severe regime.

Glinka: Russian town near Vyaz'ma named for Mikhail Ivanovich Glinka (1804-1857), the first Russian composer of international repute.

gulag: Main Directorate for Corrective Labor Camps. System of forced labor camps located in remote regions of the Soviet Union, such as the far north and Siberia.

gymnasium: In Europe and the Soviet Union, a secondary preparatory school.

Ing Idisz: Yiddish for "Yung (Young) Yiddish," an association of painters, poets and writers in Łódź, Poland

Ispolkom: Acronym for Ispolnitel'niy komitet, the executive committee of the soviet, or branch of local government in the U.S.S.R. The Soviet Union comprised many local soviets of workers' deputies. (See *soviet* below.)

JOINT: See AJJDC.

kolkhoz: Acronym for Kollektivnoe Khozyaistvo, "collective farm." Stalin's collectivization efforts called for converting all independently owned farmland either into collective farms (the *kolkhoz*) or state-owned farms (the *sovkhoz*).

komandirovka: A permit to travel for business purposes.

Komsomol: Acronym for Kommunisticheskiy Soiuz Molodyozhi, Communist Youth League, founded 1918, for youths ages 14-26 as a training ground for future Communist Party members. It supervised the other communist organizations for young people, namely the Octobrists and the Young Pioneers. It conducted many useful services under the leadership of the Communist Party besides assisting in propagating communist policies among Soviet youth. Komsomol members were also enlisted to help in various national causes such as industrialization, collectivization and the eradication of illiteracy, and also in the defense against the Nazis in WWII.

Luftwaffe: The German Air Force.

NKVD: People's Commissariat of Internal Affairs. Responsible for the detection of subversive elements, supervision of prison and labor camps, and "reeducation" of political offenders. Forerunner of the KGB.

Octobrists: Communist youth organization for the youngest children, up to age 8. Children in the Soviet Union were expected to join the Octobrists, then the Young Pioneers, and finally the Komsomol.

ORT: Renamed Society for Reconstruction through Training. Its original purpose was to provide untrained Jews of working age with a useful trade or skill. Today it is a private, nonsectarian, nonprofit organization.

pogroms: Organized massacres of Jews in Russia and Eastern Europe. They were carried out under both the Tsars and Communists under Stalin.

soviet council or *soviet*: Ostensibly, the soviets and the Communist party were separate and distinct. "Soviets" of workers' deputies were central and local legislative and executive authorities. It was the intention of the October Revolution that these groups would govern the U.S.S.R., thus giving a voice to even the smallest communities, but the soviets were really under Communist party control at all times.

Sovnarkom: Acronym for Soviet Narodnykh Komissarov, "Council of People's Commissars." In charge of supervising the soviets. See *soviet* above.

UNRRA: United Nations Relief and Rehabilitation Administration. In western Europe toward the end of World War II and afterwards, a number of resettlement centers were established to help resettle or repatriate the millions of Europeans displaced from their homes because of World War II. The first centers were run by the Allied Armies and the

Supreme Headquarters Allied Expeditionary Force (SHAEF) (1944-45); UNRRA (1945-47); and the International Refugee Organization (IRO)(1947-51).

Young Pioneers: Communist youth organization for children ages 9-13. At age 9, in the third year of elementary school, children in the USSR took a loyalty oath to communism and the Soviet Union and received a red neckerchief and badge in exchange. They helped guide the younger Octobrists and prepared themselves to be Komsomol members. In addition to political indoctrination, the organization also offered after-school activities such as arts and crafts, sewing, etc. to members.

Zionists: Members of the movement to bring back into existence a Jewish nation. It wasn't until 1897 when Hungarian journalist Theodor Herzl convened the first World Zionist Conference in Basel, Switzerland, and started Zionist organizations in countries with large Jewish populations that the dream of such a nation began to seem a real possibility. The Balfour Declaration in 1917 promised British support for a Jewish homeland in Palestine, and the mandate given to Britain in the 1920s for Palestine prepared the way, but it wasn't until after World War II that the majority of Zionists agreed to the UN plan for partitioning Palestine. On May 14, 1948 the State of Israel was proclaimed.

Zloty: Unit of Polish currency.

THE DAVIDSONS' MIGRATION
A CHRONOLOGY BY CHAPTER

1   Łódź (April 1939-September 1939)

2   Łódź (September 1939; winter 1939)

3   Hanna and mother on the road from Łódź to Soviet-occupied Poland: across the River Bug, through Zambrów-Koscielna, to Białystok, Poland (December 1939); in Białystok for some weeks, then through Vitebsk to Orsha, Byelorussia to join father (winter 1940)

4   Orsha (winter 1940 through December 31)

5   Orsha: change plans to move to Gor'kiy (Nizhniy Novgorod) after June 22, 1941; leave Orsha June 24, 1941, for Vyaz'ma; stay at a kolkhoz 20 km east of Orsha, then travel through Dubrova and Lida—near Smolensk—Byelorussian-Russian border (July), then Glinka, to Vyaz'ma; abandon plans to go to Moscow-Gor'kiy; travel through Penza, Ruzayevka, Arzamas, Zelenodol'sk (end of July 1941), Yoshkar Ola (August 7, 1941), and Toryal; arrive in Kuzhnur (August 9, 1941)

6   Kuzhnur (August 9, 1941-September 1941)

7   Kuzhnur (though Hanna boards in Toryal for school) (early September 1941-winter 1942)

8   Kuzhnur (1942-summer 1943); Yoshkar Ola (summer 1943-summer 1944)

9   Kuzhnur (summer 1944-September 1944); Hanna leaves for school in Moscow (traveling through Kazan) (September 1944-June 1945); parents move to Proskurov (now Khmel'nyts'kyy) (winter 1945)

10   Moscow (June 1945); to Proskurov (now Khmel'nyt'skyy) (June 1945-February 1946); to Łódź, through Katowice, Poland (February 1946)

11   Łódź (February 1946)

12   Łódź (February 1946-fall 1946)

13   On the road from Łódź (fall 1946): Wałbrzych, Poland (two days); Frydlant v Čechách, Czechoslovakia (five days); to a camp 15 km over the Czech border (two days); Vienna, Austria (three days); to another camp near Linz, Austria (a few days)

14   Near Linz, Austria (a few days, fall 1946)

15   Wegscheid, Austria (late fall 1946)

16   Unspecified former American army camp in the U.S. zone in Germany (late fall 1946)

17   Babenhausen, Germany (November 1946)

18   Stuttgart, Germany (late November 1946-April 1947)

19   Paris, France (April-late May 1947); by air to Mexico City through Lisbon, Portugal, and Dakar to Recife, Brazil (May 28-May 30, 1947); to Fortaleza, Brazil (May 30-31, 1947); to Belem, Brazil (May 31-June 1, 1947); to Trinidad (June 1-2, 1947); to Panama City, Panama (June 2-3, 1947); to Guatemala (June 3); arrive in Mexico City June 3, 1947

20   Mexico City (from June 3, 1947, on); Hanna marries Jaime Pankowsky (1951); Jaime leaves for Baltimore alone (July 1952)

21   Baltimore, Maryland (from late November 1952 on); Hanna's children born January 15, 1953, and January 3, 1956; Hanna moves to San Antonio, Texas (1956); Hanna becomes U.S. citizen (November 3, 1964); Hanna's parents become U.S. citizens (1976); Hanna's father dies (1989); Hanna's mother dies (1990)

INDEX

A

Abraham (Zina Davidson's husband), 104-105

Adler, Jacob (Yankel), 4

AJJDC , 148, 167, 175, 179, 184, 187, 209

American Jewish Joint Distribution Committee. *See* AJJDC

Anti-semitism, Poland, xii

Anti-semitism, Soviet Union, 63-64

Arzamas, 58

B

Babenhausen, 162-172

Belem, Brazil, 192-193

Ben-Gurion, David, 170

Białystok, x, 30, 33-34

Blaustein, Kuba, 22-23, 26

Blaustein, Runek, 22

Bobovnikov, Comrade, 53-57

Brauner, Ida, 4

Broderson, Moshe, 4

Brown, Edna, 204

Brown, Norman, 204

Bund (General Jewish Workers Bund), x-xi, 8, 34, 169, 186, 196, 203, 209

D

Davidson, David, 42-43, 112

Davidson, Fania, 42-43, 108-111, 113-115, 119-120; photo of, 7

Davidson, Frada, photo of, 6

Davidson, George, 42, 176, 199

Davidson, Hanna, photos of, ii, 9, 16, 17, 38, 84, 93, 97, 149, 168, 180, 198, 207

Davidson, Lisa, 112

Davidson, Lusia, 112-113

Davidson, Raquel, 42-43, 108-111, 113, 119; photo of, 114

Davidson, Sima, 112; photo of, 7

Davidson, Simon, bookeeper in Orsha, 35, 37; and Bund, 169; contacting his Russian family, 42-43; drafted to Polish army, 14; education, 6; life in Kuzhnur, 78-79; life in Mexico City, 196, 205; photos of, 7, 8, 180; and strangulated hernia, 52, 53; Stuttgart, 171, 175; travels to Gor'kiy, 48-49; travels to Moscow, 99, 101-108; travels to Sverdlovsk, 97; works in displaced persons camp, 166; works for Polish Repatriation